Your Complete Forecast 2018 Horoscope

Your Complete Forecast
2018
Horoscope

BEJAN DARUWALLA
With
NASTUR DARUWALLA

First published in India in 2017 by Harper Element
An imprint of HarperCollins *Publishers*

Copyright © Bejan Daruwalla 2017

P-ISBN: 978-93-5277-276-6
E-ISBN: 978-93-5277-277-3

2 4 6 8 10 9 7 5 3 1

Bejan Daruwalla asserts the moral right
to be identified as the author of this work.

The views and opinions expressed in this book are the author's own and the facts are
as reported by him, and the publishers are not in any way liable for the same.

HarperCollins *Publishers*
A-75, Sector 57, Noida, Uttar Pradesh 201301, India
1 London Bridge Street, London, SE1 9GF, United Kingdom
2 Bloor Street East, Toronto, Ontario M4W 1A8, Canada
Lvl 13, 201 Elizabeth Street (PO Box A565, NSW, 1235), Sydney
NSW 2000, Australia
195 Broadway, New York, NY 10007, USA

Typeset in 10.5/13.7 Sabon
By Saanvi Graphics, Noida

Printed and bound at
Printed at MicroPrints (India), New Delhi

Contents

ARIES

21 March–20 April

You are a natural leader thanks to your immense energy, vitality and force. In other words, you are vibrant like Virat Kohli, sing superbly like the late K.L. Saigal and you have the comic genius of Charlie Chaplin, perhaps the greatest actor ever. This is the time to gun down all opposition and yet be humble and decent to all in your moment of victory and triumph. Yes, money and loans will come to you for property, industry, housing, arts, research, hobbies, new avenues of work, romance, sex and dealings with corporates, industries and financial houses. All this will come naturally to you. Congrats!

- **Good qualities:** Abundant physical energy, courage, honesty, independence, self-reliance, resourcefulness

- **Metals:** Iron and steel

- **Perfume:** Honeysuckle

- **Advice:** Caution and patience

- **Gem:** Amethyst, coral, diamond (coral is best)

- **Colours:** Carmine, red, scarlet, pink

- **Characteristics:** Bold and brash

- **Key word:** Pioneer, leader, executive, courageous, 'me-first'

- **Main planet:** Mars

- **Element:** Fire

- **Health:** The head and face, tension, headaches, dizziness, skin eruptions, migraines, allergies, sleep problems

- **Other qualities:** active, excitable, impulsive, optimistic, open to change and new experiences

- **Great point:** impulsive, selfish but also very generous (strange mix)

- **Flowers:** Geranium, honeysuckle

- **Countries:** England, Germany, Poland

- **Trees:** All thorn-bearing trees

- **Cities:** Florence, Naples, Verona, Marseilles

Special Message from Bejan and Nastur: You are independent by nature and temperament. Top position and power can be achieved. But if you are very aggressive, blunt and brash, remember that there is a danger of a big fall from power and position. The reason is Saturn, the planet of power, duty and responsibility, is in your tenth angle of name and fame.

The challenge with this sign is lack of persistence. They can be argumentative, lack tact, and have a bad temper. Since Aries rules the head and face, these areas are considered the weakest part of the body for people under this sign. Common ailments are tension, headaches, dizziness and skin eruptions.

In fact, many Aries suffer from migraines and allergies too. Also, because they are indulgent, Aries need to be careful of easily gaining weight. It's a good thing he is so active! I must admit there are always exceptions to this rule.

Finances and loans will be available. Use them wisely. You will have much to do with investments, loans, funds, trusts, taxes, buildings and construction, inheritance and legacy, charitable causes, religious rites and ceremonies and pujas, tantra and mantra, prayers for the living and the dead. Take care of your health from May to July and also March. On the positive side, during the months of February, April, June, August, October and December you will be at your brilliant best. Health of parents, boss, elders will be cause for worry and concern. Take care of their health please. Overall position, power, success, loans, funds, investments, good money.

In 2018 you will have pelf and power for the simple reason that Saturn, planet of responsibility and duty, will be in your tenth angle as per Western astrology. Just for your information, Saturn will be in your tenth angle till 19 December 2020. Your symbol is the ram. The ram always climbs upwards till it reaches the top of the mountain. In the same way, you will also continue to climb till 19 December 2020. Therefore, your hard work and intensity will be well rewarded. But please try to be humble, kind, forgiving, and do not make a mountain of a molehill. That means do not take small matters to heart and do not fight over it. Save your energy for the big occasions in your life. Ganesha says this is the best advice you will ever get.

Mars is your main planet. Mars will help you tremendously from 29 January to 10 March 2017, 21 July to 5 September 2017, 17 January 2018 to 17 March 2018, 27 May 2018 to

27 June 2018, 12 September 2018 to 16 November 2018. Mars will help you in terms of energy, action, achievements and loans, funds, investments. These are your months of power, name and fame. Ganesha says please use it wisely and well and remember that in life moderation is the key to great success and even greater joy and happiness.

Ganesha says you will achieve much in your work area. Yes, loans, funds, finances and pension will be available to you. Also, your earning capacity will increase. But there is also a possibility of sudden changes in your personal and work area. This is not a contradiction. The reason is life is not simple and clear and everything does not fall into the place you want to. Life is often mysterious, has many changes and circumstances and therefore we human beings must learn to adjust to it. That is the real secret of lasting happiness. Luckily you Arians are born leaders, very brave and courageous, and therefore you will be able to fight life and come out a winner. My final word is you will be victorious if you are not very aggressive and violent. You can assert yourself but sometimes you must learn to listen to others. By doing so, you will be happy and make others happy. That is what life is all about.

JUPITER

Jupiter in your eighth angle will have the following spin-offs: Loans, funds, joint finance, insurance, legacy and legal matters, money from different sources such as rents, rentals, lottery and hidden treasure. That does sound interesting!

Tantra and mantra, high passion and sizzling sex, taxes, real estate issues, keeping your mouth shut (otherwise there's trouble), and religious rites are indicated. Jupiter helps you get money. That's important. This same time span will also be mighty important for: a) buying/selling/renovation/decoration of house, home/shop/godown/warehouse/office and so on. Let me know, dear readers, how right I am on these counts—matters to do with inheritances, wills, codicils, estate and taxes, hundis, taking care of both health and money, cooperating with other workers, finding new sources of money and profit, maintaining secrets and confidentiality, learning to use your energies carefully and not wasting or draining it away. Finally, it is most important that you should use your talents and imagination completely.

With Jupiter in your eighth angle the other main features will be: a) The focus – sharp and clear – is on joint finance, loans, public trusts and charity institution; b) Your health and that of your near and dear ones could pose some problems for you; c) A home away from home is likely; d) Problems of legacy, dowry, hidden treasures, wills, codicils, legal documents pertaining to marriage, alimony, company laws, contracts regarding corporations, bonds, funds may crop up; e) Tax matters related to land, building, shop, office, godown, warehouse and so on are to be taken care of; f) The danger of low vitality, poor health, accidents, operations, wounds, injuries – once again, I must stress health concerns; g) Lawsuits and court proceedings will have to be dealt with; h) Also, perhaps blackmail and deceit. Jupiter will be in your eighth angle from 10 October 2017 to 8 November 2018.

SATURN

By Western astrology Saturn will be in your tenth angle from 21 December 2017 to 22 March 2020. Therefore, it will apply to all Arians in both 2018 and 2019. Here are the details:

Saturn in your work slot prods you into probing at your career and business possibilities and outstanding success can be anticipated. Ganesha says, it is time to go all out for the kill. It could well be the time for awards and rewards for your services rendered, and for the efforts put in by you. Yes, your prestige will also soar. Your parents and kinsmen will be proud of you. Sounds good.

Saturn will be at the zenith or mid-heaven in your solar-scope. The results will be:

a) You will have to walk the talk. In other words, your words must match your actions. You can be aggressive but never abusive. You must lead without crushing the opinions of others.

b) You will meet influential people who will be able to help you.

c) The health of parents, elders, in-laws will make you anxious and worried.

d) There will be a great struggle for power, position and prestige. If you push too hard, you might take a big tumble.

e) If you neglect your home and family, you will finally suffer the consequences.

f) The law of karma will certainly operate for you. Remember, the Gita says, 'He who knows for certain that happiness and misery, birth and death are due to the effect of past actions, does not find anything to accomplish, and thus becomes free from care and is not attached, even though engaged in action.'

This is how Saturn will work for you in 2018:

a) Prestige, power, position, perks, pelf – the five Ps – you will achieve them all.

b) Responsibility in irreversible, monumental proportions will be almost thrust upon you, but that will give you authority and the ability to handle pressure; and that's ultimately important.

c) Prestige takes an immense leap; parents will figure in your scheme of things; inheritance and possessions will play a large role in your personal life; and you will learn to play spectacularly with all the latest gadgets and media of communication.

d) The health of parents and older people, in-laws, could be a cause of anxiety. This will go for your boss and superior too.

e) Both your proficiency and your performance will be at an all-time high and this should give you the necessary self-belief, confidence to achieve targets and goals. Helping you do this is what astrology is all about.

f) Honours, awards, rewards sum it up nicely.

g) Wish-fulfilment and hope – without this nothing is possible.

h) Food for the body, good health, good money; food for the mind, intellectual stimuli, food for the soul, spirituality and the sayings of the gurus – all these are important for you.

i) Old acquaintances, new friends, sweethearts and loved ones, mate and companions, all form a full circle of contentment and joy for you – for the most part.

j) Your income could come from more than one source. For this, one of the secrets would be mixing with people, socializing and fraternizing, in short, networking as they now say. Otherwise also, Saturn in this position is ideally placed for achieving this, quite paradoxically.

k) Recognition and acknowledgements of worth will come to you, and that will obviously be sweet and satisfying.

l) You must learn not to offend those who love and support you. Not ego, but love, will put you where you aspire to be.

m) Possessions, combining substance with style, in clothes, work, home, renovation/decoration of either new or ancestral property is foretold.

n) Good news about children, and romance and hobbies and sports have a great significance for you.

o) Pious deeds, charitable acts, the elder brother, paternal uncle, the longevity of your mother, finding lost/stolen goods/valuables, treasures, lotteries and windfalls, recovery from illness and therefore, returning from hospital or medical centres, are the other vital features. Quite a handful!

URANUS

Till 16 May 2018, Uranus will be in Aries. In other words, Uranus will be in your sign. Uranus is the planet of both revolution and evolution. Therefore, there will be big changes in your personal life very specially and this will have an effect on your profession, business and job. I personally believe that though you may feel unsettled and restless you will finally accept all the changes which circumstances bring about for you. In the long run these changes will certainly help you. From 18 May 2018, Uranus will be in your second house of finance and family. Uranus will be responsible for sudden gains and losses. It will have the greatest impact on your finances and funds. There could be a change in the nature of your job, profession or business. If it is so, do not worry. At the same time, I wish to make it clear that astrologers are not gods and what I have said about the outer planets Pluto, Neptune and Uranus may not have the full impact of what I have predicted. The other reason is that these outer planets influence countries more than individuals. Therefore, please do not worry overmuch.

NEPTUNE

Neptune will be in your twelfth angle till 28 January 2026. Therefore, Neptune's influence will be felt in 2018. Neptune will give you inspiration, imagination. But Neptune will also result in expenses, ill health, false accusations and possibly lawsuits and illicit relationships. In short, Neptune will bring out the best and the worst in you. Beware of being cheated or of cheating others in every possible way, namely, money, women, relationships, drugs, drinks, conning and even smuggling. But Neptune can lead you to genuine spirituality, love of God and nature and also service to the people of the world. In short Neptune is a double-edged sword specially for you Arians in 2018.

PLUTO

Till March 2023, Pluto, the power planet, will be in your tenth angle. It is very clear that this will apply to you in both 2018 and 2019. Pluto will help you achieve name and fame, recognition and rewards. In short, Pluto, like our own Virat Kohli, will bat for you in the game of life itself. I am sure you understand the value and worth of it.

MONTHLY ROUND-UP

January: Up and about, hard work, you will be ready to be on the go, be it home/office. **February**: Fun and games, friendship and fraternity, gains and gaiety. **March**: Too many things happening all together; see that you conserve your energy/vitality. **April**: Month of progress, prosperity, pelf and getting things done. **May**: Loans and funds and deals and transactions, buying/selling. **June**: Assignments, communication, transport, ties, trips, relatives. **July**: Home, house, family, shopping, renovation, decoration, alteration. **August**: Trips, ceremonies, rites, name and fame, future plans. **September**: Work, health, rewards, service, pets, projects, colleagues, promotion. **October**: Love, marriage, lawsuits, relationships, travel, contracts, communication, enemies. **November**: Joint finance, loans, funds, immigration, moving, shifting, capital formation, passion, sex. **December**: Joy, publicity, travel, ceremony, functions, parties, invitations, import and export, collaboration, contacts and happiness because of abundance.

HAPPINESS QUOTA: 80 per cent

WEEKLY REVIEW (BY PHASES OF THE MOON)

2 January: Full Moon in Cancer

Home, health, family matters, even concerns regarding family health or finances, or both, could be more than demanding. You may feel that the pace in the millennium is truly hectic. Go for it, Arians, but don't trample over the dreams of others. Take it slow and easy and, for Ganesha's sake, take some time off.

8 January: Last Quarter in Libra

Entertainment, amusement, hobbies and creative pursuits are all favoured, along with speculation and investing in the right places. It's a time for care and caution in money matters, or with regard to valuables, documents, wills, certificates. Don't be too open about revealing your hand, even to friends. That's not the way to play the poker game of life.

17 January: New Moon in Capricorn

It's time to work hard and play your cards well, make the right moves. The three Ps – power, position and your personal angle – are all in focus, after the Sun–Saturn trine of 1 January. It's a marvellous placing, and this is what it brings you. Of course, you will have to stretch yourself in many directions. Just don't spread yourself too thin.

24 January: First Quarter in Taurus

On the one hand, possessions, property, acquisitions and on the other, a higher consciousness or plane of existence. Spiritual journeys, or even actual travel to distant places, trade, export–import and of course, in today's world, communicating at all levels. Achievements made now will give a different kind of satisfaction.

31 January: Full Moon in Leo

The moon's quarter in the last period of your sun sign ushered in hectic activity. Thus, now it extends to include finance; funds, buying, selling, investments, financial planning for the millennium are the name of the game. Don't go overboard, weigh your options before making long-term commitments/plans regarding money.

7 February: Last Quarter in Scorpio

Finance, finance and finance thrice. That's the scene this week, be it household expenses, outlay in business or both – anything that touches the pocket or the purse strings. In the process, you may well pick up some possessions, fun articles, even some gadgets. You learn to juggle finances well indeed!

15 February: New Moon in Aquarius

Chancing your arm, backing the throw of the dice in matters, financial (speculation) bull runs on the stock market, if you're a major player, and also chancing your heart. You're in the right mood for both. Optimism and confidence at an all-time high.

23 February: First Quarter in Gemini

An inner search, looking for the Godhead within us all or the Buddha-like nirvana is balanced, strangely enough, with getting on in social mobility (upward, of course, I said 'yuppy', didn't I?). You'll have to devote extra time and attention to money matters, definitely.

2 March: Full Moon in Virgo

A wish-fulfilment, much fun and games, even hectic socializing and yet, strange as it may seem, at the same time a search for inner values, the real you that you don't always show to the world. Love and hatred – two sides of the same coin – may both be experienced, in relationships, even in social interaction or family matters. Learning to cope is one way of strengthening your personality, Ganesha says.

9 March: Last Quarter in Sagittarius

Now it's not social/familial/kinship relationships that are important but those with superiors and bosses, officials and authorities and subordinates, employees. You still need to watch the interests of the first named, though. Funds will flow in, loans and resources will be organized very smoothly, and so also will the contacts and communications trend.

17 March: New Moon in Pisces

Awards, rewards, recognition, appreciation and the benefits that come with them. Health problems of older relatives, parents, perhaps even your boss, may cause anxious moments. So also having to take disciplinary action, or inflict punishments. Perhaps at work, or in a social context. Position and power bring their own responsibility after all.

24 March: First Quarter in Cancer

A time when you may be attempted to be uncooperative, even harsh in your dealings with people. Financial gains come your way, but don't look for the quick buck. It's got to be the just rewards of your own efforts. Correspondence, short trips and ties will be highlighted in this period. Even shopping trips, where you're tempted to blow up some cash on trifles, fun purchases, fripperies.

31 March: Full Moon in Libra

The monthly trend, with the moon in your sign – you will make great individual advances, but will have a tendency to pander to your own ego and pride. That won't augur well for personal and professional relationships, both of which are highlighted in this period. Some important decisions will be made, based on intellectual and career needs as well as purely personal considerations.

8 April: Last Quarter in Capricorn

Partnerships, law, legal cases, buying/selling (may be of property or assets), getting a commission are highlighted. Also, buildings, construction or even doing up the house. Your own interests and concerns will be paramount, but not in a selfish way. It's just that you'll watch out for yourself, your family, your home, and you will be more than active in these spheres.

16 April: New Moon in Aries

Both business and pleasure will be motivating factors in this period. Business partnerships as well as personal ones will therefore be equally important. Love, romance, friends, passionate interludes will all yield the 'pleasure principle'. You might even have a field day at sports, if that's where your pleasure lies.

22 April: First Quarter in Leo

Worries about the health of older relatives, parents, even superiors will make you work harder than usual. Stress should be avoided, therefore. It's a time when your true worth, efforts, sterling qualities will all be recognized, appreciated, even rewarded. Happy times with family and kin can happen too, but it's not a time for forcing issues or having confrontations.

30 April: Full Moon in Scorpio

As I've frequently pointed out, the trend for the lunar month is usually ushered in by the new period. It will be finances – so far on the back burner – that occupy your time, energy, talents and, more so, contracts, memoranda of understanding, agreements, joint finance. Also important will be a makeover in terms of clothes, jewellery, fashion accessories, make-up, a new look – and you'll go out and 'shop till you drop'.

8 May: Last Quarter in Aquarius

Amusements, entertaining and being feted, wined and dined, playtime with children, friends, loved ones all come together to give you a wonderful time recreation-wise. Also, a good time for making some 'fast money'. Thrilling romance too. I would say, excitement in different ways sums it up.

15 May: New Moon in Taurus

Once again, money and honey, romance and finance! Love will almost definitely be of the earthly, sensual, passionate variety, not 'the meeting of two minds' immortalized by Shakespeare. You may have a gift, legacy, windfall; unexpected gambles can pay off. It's a lucky time for securing loans, credit, leasing and even for paying off old debts.

22 May: First Quarter in Virgo

The theme of love continues, and once again it's time for pleasure in each other's company – joy, a celebration of life itself. You are active not just emotionally/passionately but also at work, making the right moves, the right decisions. Money matters will be more or less smooth, so all in all, a good period by the grace of Ganesha!

29 May: Full Moon in Sagittarius

Connections, contacts (whether long-distance or direct), even calls, letters, faxes, email. Communication and information are the name of the game now. Those in the electronic and print media, in information technology, the creative arts will find this period full of promise and gains. People and places are now part of your own backyard, and so also ties with your environment.

6 June: Last Quarter in Pisces

Higher studies, research, higher learning, idealism, dabbling in the occult and spiritual. You'll be existing on a much more elevated level of consciousness, and very actively so. There may be journeys, either spiritual or actual, from which you will gain either a pilgrimage or a study tour, business travel, foreign conferences, seminars and such.

13 June: New Moon in Gemini

You will be very focussed on the goals you have been thinking about achieving. Whether you achieve them or not is another matter, but you will know where you're going. I must point out that if these goals are not realistic, you may experience a sense of defeat, sorrow or even depression.

20 June: First Quarter in Virgo

A resurgence of hope and determination, a sense of purpose, comes to you in this period of your own sign. You experience both aggression and love, pleasure, and go out to seek them in all that you do. Money matters, domestic issues find you resolute yet charming.

28 June: Full Moon in Capricorn

It's home, family, the comforts of your hearth, your castle that you enjoy. Parents and children are in harmony with you. There may be family gatherings or outings or even perhaps a short journey to visit dear ones. Money matters will be smooth, but not spectacular. So also your health. A good time to let others do the thinking and talking, even the decision making.

6 July: Last Quarter in Aries

You want to start afresh, particularly in terms of career goals and attitudes to both profession and home. A stronger faith in yourself, more objectivity, all help, you give your best shot to your work, impervious to rivals and competitors, like Arjuna was instructed to do by Krishna in the Bhagavadgita. And you do experience much satisfaction in doing so. Ganesha sees to it.

13 July: New Moon in Cancer

You look at yourself in the mirror of life very closely indeed and the important thing is, you want to like what you see. Self-improvement, physical fitness, beautification, even new make-up/hairstyle/clothes, will be spent on, both in money and in effort. You may even join a gym, sport, some health club on your way to what you consider a better you. There may also be bond, partnership, marriage, being part of a team.

19 July: First Quarter in Libra

Libra is the opposite number for Aries – the sign you get on with. Here it means that you attain a certain balance in your life – home and office, work and pleasure, vocation and avocation. In personal relationships and in your marriage too, you appreciate the value of give and take as a means for promotion of harmony, particularly in money matters.

27 July: Full Moon in Aquarius

Creativity at white heat – the arts, the media, public relations, copywriting, even children and hobbies. It's a time when even procreation and a new birth are favoured. It could equally be a good time to start a new project, launch a new product, undertake a new venture. Romance too could well be the new venture. And I'm not joking. I just see you marching to a very different drummer.

4 August: Last Quarter in Taurus

It's back to the world of finance, money, willy-nilly. I wonder if people even stop to think what this phrase 'willy-nilly' implies – whether of your own will or against it. That's exactly it for you. Funds, joint finances, debts, even loans for the future will keep you more than busy whereas you will feel an urge for seclusion, renouncing the world, taking up meditation/worship/tantra/mantra/prayer. Ganesha will guide you

11 August: New Moon in Leo

A time when you'll get work done, call in favours, get results, see your efforts bearing fruit. You might be excused for feeling complacent, but that's not a good thing. Humility, charm, willingness to help will serve you better. Your popularity graph soars, so also do your spirits. You are fun to be with and there are lots of opportunities for fun and entertainment coming your way right now.

18 August: First Quarter in Scorpio

More of the same, a refill of the cocktail of the two Fs of fun and finance see you through this period as well. On the financial front, it's funds, taxes, rentals, leases, some mergers or tie-ups and fun. I hope I don't need to spell it out. It's a rare meeting of all that's best for you around this time and even business and professional interactions/meetings acquire a personal slant.

26 August: Full Moon in Pisces

It's others that you will be totally concerned with during this period and even at some cost to yourself. Social welfare, community projects and concerns, care of older people, pets, subordinates, dependents are all important. There may be a bit of change, reorganization and revamping done at work as well, but there are no hard feelings generated. You're god with people right now.

3 September: Last Quarter in Gemini

Group activities, being part of a larger social order, organization, conferences, TV shows – all the things that make you part of the wide world vision that is almost part of you now. Into this, add the spice of higher study, original research, philosophical insights, and you've got a rare mixture. Ethical values too will be important.

9 September: New Moon in Virgo

All the philosophy, ethics, higher values that you were interested in during the last period now crystallize into a mood of inner peace, soul searching, even metaphysical questions and esoteric insights into the art of living, if so inclined. Your concern and love for your fellow beings will be the guiding light, the raison d'être of your life.

16 September: First Quarter in Sagittarius

It's time to travel and on the higher plane of intellectualism, if no other way. Trips will be as important to you as ties. And the ties will be those of love, matrimony, kinship, social commitment, the community – the entire gamut! You will want to communicate and commune with everything around you – even Nature!

25 September: Full Moon in Aries

All kinds of relationship will be important in this period and through the entire coming period. New bonds, ties, relationships can be forged ranging from an engagement or wedding to business or legal partnerships. Your own attitude of cooperation and conciliation will make this possible. It will make you efficient at work, and easier to get on with in general.

2 October: Last Quarter in Cancer

The spirit of teamwork and cooperation has you firing on all cylinders, ready to go for the kill. I mean this in terms of getting results in office concerns, domestic matters. Love and romance are another story, not so ardently followed. It's work that's all-important, and that too for its own sake, not for the monetary rewards.

9 October: New Moon in Libra

Your own sign, once again. You will put yourself on centre stage and all things that touch your life and your self-image will be emphasized during this period – your job, home, relationships, even appearance and clothes/outfits, accessories, hairdo. The works, in short. And they will all click, so that it's a time for wish-fulfilment.

16 October: First Quarter in Capricorn

Work and home are the twin engines of the spacecraft on which you zoom into orbit. You don't let up at all on the work front and add on all possible care for your home, family, your house, even your parents, ancestors, distant relatives. It's your own world that you seek to create and inhabit. And earn for too, adds Ganesha.

24 October: Full Moon in Taurus

Two different sources of power for you now. On the material level, it's money matters like loans, funds, trade, capital formation, market, share, investments. The other is the world of sorcerer and spirits of life after death, of souls in Purgatory, perhaps even the planchette or the Ouija board as you dabble in the occult and the tantric aspect of religion.

31 October: Last Quarter in Leo

After the mental stimulation and activity you have experienced, it's 'relax or burst' time. And relax you do, with a vengeance, letting your hair down. Romance, partying, dancing to the exotic beat of calypso/jazz/reggae/soul/hard rock, whatever gives you the most fun.

7 November: New Moon in Scorpio

With your batteries recharged, your stamina restored after having called 'time out', you're back at work! Arians have this great capacity to remain focused on their own interests and pursuits. And for you it's: a) money, income generation, rentals and property, acquiring assets that will pay handsomely later and b) making friends, making up, making love, whatever is necessary to heal the wounds of the past and make life sweet for your loved ones.

15 November: First Quarter in Aquarius

Ganesha says progress and achievements come to you now. Your contacts, colleagues, companions are a source of strength, ideas, support. You may not suffer from a dearth of ideas, but bouncing them off wise, equally aware people always helps. Your ideas get polished, sharpened and acquire a cutting edge. In addition to these good connections, a truly beneficial and solid partnership could develop now, so that there is mutual gain and also shared respect and regard.

23 November: Full Moon in Gemini

The love, care, concern that you aspire for (as do we all) are yours in full measure. In fact, your 'cup runneth over' with joy and warmth in relationships, family bonding, friendship. There may be the added thrill of joy from your children, a wedding to be held soon, or an engagement announced. Sports and adventure too.

30 November: Last Quarter in Virgo

It's you dancing down the streets with joyous abandon or laughing all the way to the bank. That is the vision that Ganesha conjures up before me. He adds a note of warning, as always. Don't throw caution to the winds in your elation and euphoria. Take care of your health and your purse.

7 December: New Moon in Sagittarius

It's time for larger concerns now. You have a certain sense of security in your home, your family, your income-generating ability. You now turn to: a) spiritual and occult practices; b) social and charitable concerns, working for the public good; c) healing and nurturing others and in so doing nurturing your higher self, so that there is calm and certainty where there were doubts and anxieties.

15 December: First Quarter in Pisces

It's time for action, but a vastly different kind. All the C words – communications, connections abroad, contacts, computer technology – come together to form a single unit – creativity – and that too, truly with a capital C. All the media, all forms of self-expression, all the creative arts – you choose your own special forte and perform brilliantly and effectively.

22 December: Full Moon in Cancer

It's time for you to get to work. And working with a will, can the rewards, recognition, results be far behind? The beauty of it all is that it's not the rewards that attract you but an inner satisfaction; the glow that comes from a job well done lights up your life in many ways. And that is the gift of the new millennium for you.

29 December: Last Quarter in Libra

The year 2018 is drawing to a close and new trends for 2019 will be ushered in. It's a time when you realize that though heaven always exceeds a man's grasp (by definition it should be so) but the joy of reaching for the stars is not possible without hard, even unremitting, work and toil. And the rewards are bound to be there. As you have found for yourself, from more or less happy experience over the past period, by the grace of Ganesha.

Taurus

21 April–21 May

Ganesha says, the length of the annual forecast will not be the same. We are not selling vegetables per kilo. Every sign has different needs and demands. Therefore, the length will depend upon it.

- **Colours:** Earth tones, green, orange, yellow
- **Colours that promote love, romance and social harmony:** Red-violet, violet
- **Colours that promote earning power:** Yellow, yellow-orange.
- **Gems:** Coral, emerald
- **Metal:** Copper
- **Scents:** Bitter almond, rose, vanilla, violet
- **Quality:** Stability
- **Quality most needed for balance:** Flexibility
- **Strongest virtues:** Endurance, loyalty, patience, stability, a harmonious disposition
- **Deepest needs:** Comfort, material ease, wealth

- **Characteristics to avoid:** Rigidity, stubbornness, tendency to be overly possessed and materialistic

Special Message from Bejan and Nastur: I have given great importance to colours and food and beauty in the above salient features because you Taureans are all about colours + food + beauty + money. This is pure digital.

Taurus shows love by gifts and cheques and sometimes showers money as if from heaven. Comfort loving, food and clothes and a jolly good life makes him happy. Taurus is a child with a candy. Love him. Touch him. Kiss him. Massage him. Make him hear music and he will be your pet. Sometimes he is stubborn. Then just let him be. Finally, he will get over it and grasp your hands lovingly. There you go, as the Americans say, three cheers!

JUPITER

One major advantage of Jupiter in the seventh house is that whenever there is any problem, which might involve, besides other things, a monetary angle, the family of the spouse comes forward to extend some monetary help and all other kinds of support to the individual.

By Vedic astrology, the seventh angle or house stands for the spouse, sex partner, marriage, adultery, lust or passion, nature and character of spouse, sexual union, secret love affairs, journeys, deviation from one's path, partnership in business, overt enemies, quarrels, theft, loss of memory, recovery of lost wealth, progress, attainment of status, the grandfather, brother's son and death. In medical astrology: lower urinary tract, anal canal, semen, urethra, prostate, the sexual act.

Ganesha says, the Fs of fame, fortune, fancies and freebies will be yours. You will be in the news as well as make news! 'Fame is the perfume of heroic needs,' said the great philosopher Socrates. And who are we to dispute him? Fame is the magnifying glass of life itself!

Why have I accentuated the fame angle? For two reasons. First, it is the time, the right time, for you to be popular and as I always say, astrology is all about timing. You deserve it. Secondly, Jupiter the planet of prosperity and pelf, will be in your seventh angle of relationships at every level. I might add that modern astrology is all about relationships and behaviour pattern, since we have realized their value, relevance and importance as never before.

How come this paean of praise and prediction? Jupiter, the planet of plenty, prosperity and wisdom (a rare mix) whirls away in your seventh angle of achievements and approbation. The seventh angle signifies:

a) Connections, contacts, reaching out to people and places;

b) Journeys, ceremonies, legal matters;

c) Public relationships and competitions, change of locale/ surroundings;

d) Collaborations and cooperation, wedding/engagement;

e) Blowing hot and cold in relationships.

Jupiter in seventh angle means it could be a live-in relationship, a permanent attachment, a mighty bonding. Ganesha says, now you know the real impact of Jupiter in your angle.

The other significant features of Jupiter in your seventh angle will cover:

1. Change of locale,
2. Contests,
3. Sales and PR,
4. Marketing and distribution
5. Opening of new branches,
6. Expansion at all levels,
7. Being flexible and accommodating, more accepting of views other than your tenacious but understanding and sympathetic.

I admit openly that sometimes I go wrong, but that's the likelihood I see.

SATURN

Saturn, the planet of responsibility will be in your ninth angle of luck, love, laughter from 21 December 2017 to 22 March 2020. The spin and shine will result in the following: a) Mood elevation, publicity, ceremony, evolution of the spirit; b) Research and higher learning, real wisdom, long-distance journeys and connections; c) Parents, elders, in-laws will figure very prominently in your scheme of things, and there's some danger to their health and well-being. Therefore, a medical check-up would be a good idea, and remember, it is merely a suggestion; d) Future plans and even mighty campaigns will be planned and that's the heart of the matter; e) You will be dealing with in-laws and relatives quite intimately, and prayers for the living and the dead, dreams about them, as well as rare insights, could make it interesting; f) Try to seek approval of your programme instead of riding the high horse and making others feel small and inferior. I mean don't be on an ego trip. Rather, get results in your favour. Believe me, this is good, practical common-sense advice; g) Name and fame, the vistas of your horizon, will open out splendidly and that's the open sesame, the mantra to power and knowledge: a rare combination. Your hand will be on the level of power, but your mind will compute information and make it come wondrously alive. Writers, teachers, method specialists, idea persons, journalists, professors, religious heads, psychics, very definitely lawyers and surgeons and physicians and scientists and mathematicians – the quintet of five as I call them – could well make a world splash! Yes, that's how good it is; h) Be responsible, understanding and generous, if you want to be deeply appreciated and highly respected – and that's the truth.

VENUS

Venus, your main planet, will be in your sign from 31 March to 24 April 2018. This will help you in terms of both romance and finance. Venus will also favour you in journeys and communication from 11 February to 6 March and again from 1 to 17 January very specially. The best part of it is in July; Venus will help you in million different ways. But specially in terms of children, hobbies, sports, creativity and in all games of chance. From 9 September to 31 October once again you will love and be loved and your heart will sing like a nightingale. Yes, marriage is on the cards. From 3 December 2018, right up to 6 January 2019, you will steal the show and also the heart of your loved ones. Wow!

URANUS

Uranus will bring about conditions which require expenses, health care and hospitalization of your near ones. Disturbances are likely in matters of your loved ones, family, friends. The simple truth is nobody in life gets everything. We all have to face a few mishaps, hazards and difficult times. But very possibly 2018 will be your year, Taureans.

NEPTUNE

Neptune, the outer planet will help you in all creative pursuits and very specially music, drama, poetry, painting, acting, sculpture, jewellery, designs. The best part of it is you will make money from it.

PLUTO

Pluto will aid you in getting a handle on things. In simple English, you will be able to control matters to your liking. This simple sentence explains everything.

MONTHLY ROUND-UPS

January: Three Cs, contacts, communication, computers; **February**: Home, house, parents, in-laws, property, retirement for the elderly, foundations for new projects; **March**: Entertainment, love, engagement, hobbies, sports, games of chance; in a word, creativity; **April**: Health, employment, pets, subordinates, colleagues, debts and funds; **May**: Marriage, legal issues, friends and enemies, trips and ties, collaborations, competition; it is a mixed bag; **June**: Money, passion, joint finance, buying, selling, shopping, taxes, real estate, insurance, focusing on health and strain and drain (on the purse and perhaps on you physically); **July**: Leapfrog to fame, publicity, spirituality, fulfilment, journey, education, future plans, relations; **August**: Tough decisions, health of elders, parents, in-laws, work pressures absolutely tremendous, issues of prestige and status are possible; **September**: Friendship, the social whirl, romance, material gains, hopes, desires, ambition; happy days are here again; **October**: Expenses, losses, contacts, love, secret deals, journeys, spirituality – a paradox, a big contradiction; **November**: Confidence, power, gains, happiness, right timing, the realization of wishes; **December**: Finances, food, family, taxes, buying, selling, shopping, property, functions and meets. You will be a crowd puller! That's great.

HAPPINESS QUOTA: 85 per cent

WEEKLY REVIEW (BY PHASES OF THE MOON)

2 January: Full Moon in Cancer

You've set the pace from the word 'go'. It is on several fronts that you'll be working hard, in fact even going all out to achieve your own goals. Your career, communication and interaction with people (not personally, not professionally, but a mixture of both) and of course, your personal relationships at which you'll be intense, even demanding.

8 January: Last Quarter in Libra

A tremendous rise in status, social position, prestige and also in getting on with people. You can be charming, but are also inclined to bludgeon in, occasionally, in their determination to get their own way. You will need to soften, to tone down the image you project, especially in meetings, interviews and conferences, and learn the gentle art of truly communicating, rather than performing at it!

17 January: New Moon in Capricorn

You're restless, at sixes and sevens with yourself in several ways, in fact even ready to gamble with life itself, take chances. In moderation, of course, you just may meet with success in your attempts, if the risks that you take are not just calculated but carefully thought out as a strategy for living. You need to build bridges – travel, communication technology, personal one-to-one interaction with people.

24 January: First Quarter in Taurus

It's time for personal interaction, not clashes of personality, particularly with your boss, superiors, officials, even colleagues and subordinates. Not a good time to be a bull in a china shop, dear Taureans. Finesse is the name of the game – even in higher studies, research and development, training modules, discussion groups. For these last mentioned, travel is also likely, not to mention good money prospects.

31 January: Full Moon in Leo

You will set your own targets and work like a Trojan to achieve them. The results could easily be spectacular success at money matters, property issues, even renovation/alteration of your home, domestic squabbles. It's your focused attitude that helps but you're going to be spectacularly busy, obviously. And Ganesha reminds you, it's a trend for the period to come.

7 February: Last Quarter in Scorpio

In your own birth sign all activities and emotions get greatly heightened and there will be an intensity in all you do, think, experience. There will be a marvellous inflow of cash, and funds and loans will come through for new projects. You may also acquire some new gadgets for home/office that will add to your comfort and efficiency – like a new dishwasher or the latest hardware for the office.

15 February: New Moon in Aquarius

Having got where you wanted in terms of career/business/ better employment, it's time to relax, unwind, party and socialize, and you love it! Even hobbies, children, some new skill will give pleasure now, and pay off later. So also romance, love affairs and even blind dates – an outmoded concept now, but they can still happen.

23 February: First Quarter in Gemini

It's a time when your mind is becalmed and contended enough to turn to higher things like faith, religion, tantra and mantra, prayer, yoga – any or all of the above. You will experience a change in your inner values, a moving on from typical Taurean materialism to more spiritual, more humanitarian, even more New Age values, if they attract you.

2 March: Full Moon in Virgo

Once again, a time of unusual, even frenetic activity dawns. There will be a lot of expenses, perhaps some entertaining, giving of gifts, handouts, tips and largesse. It's certain that you'll be spending on these things, but in the process, you do have a whale of a time. Parties and outings galore!

9 March: Last Quarter in Sagittarius

A unique placing, which is reflected in your mood and mindset. With heavy socializing and personal interaction will come a desire for solitude, quietness of mind and spirit. You may actually enjoy the 'lonely in a crowd' feeling. Some rivalry, or open animosity may be experienced and could well trigger off this feeling.

17 March: New Moon in Pisces

The trend of the last period continues, but while you're having fun, dancing into the wee hours, you're probably thinking of just how shallow such pleasures can see, or perhaps searching for more lasting values, a better self, a better way to live and love. A phase of enlightenment, deep faith, that runs like a vein of gold in your life.

24 March: First Quarter in Cancer

You will be drawn to social and charitable activities and concerns. Perhaps the result of the awakening of your higher self that you have been experiencing in the immediate past. You may be inspired to make a major job switch, even change of profession or career. Expenses will outstrip income and some economizing may prove unavoidable. Some private matters, even secret ones, may have to be sorted out now, but they will no longer hamper your progress.

31 March: Full Moon in Libra

There could have been a feeling that things are not going your way, or at least that there are many obstacles in your journey through life. You will have to restrain yourself – temper, pride, impatience all to be kept in check. Expenses will be very high, and there could be health problems to cope with too. A difficult period to get through, you will have problems before things ease off, but ease they will. That's Ganesha's promise.

8 April: Last Quarter in Capricorn

You have to sort out problems at home, even deal with things like the repair of gadgets, leaking roofs, whatever. Once again, unforeseen expenses to deal with. Your parents, dependents and pets too will have to be cared for, or have an illness. Taureans can be calm in moments of crisis – and that's what you might need to do now.

16 April: New Moon in Aries

My old faithful phrase 'trips and ties' sums up this period. Journeys will be important – so also legal issues, perhaps a partnerships or collaboration. Personal relationships will thankfully be pleasant so that you can concentrate on work. That's also because you're ready and willing to fulfil commitments to family and kin, even though costs/expenses may be rather high.

22 April: First Quarter in Leo

Some matters will drag inconclusively, causing you a fair amount of anxiety. You will set a hectic pace, run like the wind – be it heavy industries, journey, trips, pilgrimages, tour, enlisting in clubs and organizations, cleaning up your image and that of the company you represent, religious impulses and spiritual experiences, publicity, ceremony, rites, fun and fanfare, ads, computers and electronics – for reaching out to people and places.

30 April: Full Moon in Scorpio

Your birth month, and the moon in your own sign usher in a more favourable phase. Some happy times to be enjoyed, so that eating out, dressing up for parties, acquiring some new clothes/jewels, at least much more cash – freedom are the things that help. And it may well get better as the month progresses. Give thanks to Ganesha.

8 May: Last Quarter in Aquarius

You may now realize that you've been neglecting your family and projects as you partied the night away, but it's not too late to make amends. You'll have to rethink the financial scene and pay extra attention to partnerships, collaborations that you have been trying to start earlier and had put on the back burner. Publicity and media-related activities will prosper.

15 May: New Moon in Taurus

Your popularity, market worth, even your credit will all soar upwards. And you are ready to give thanks where it is due – to Ganesha, of course. You don't have to be pushy and stubborn any more. Gentle, friendly persuasion will get better results. Past hassles will have to be sorted out, with a tactful attitude, so that you can progress beyond them.

22 May: First Quarter in Virgo

Your self-confidence soars. I might be excused in calling it daring, even effrontery. It will make you more caring, more willing to listen, now that things are going your way. Actions taken now will change your life for the better. Also, add to your image in the eyes of others, especially loved ones.

29 May: Full Moon in Sagittarius

An upsurge, a soaring graph in all your activities, but the focus will be money, finances, filthy lucre – whatever you choose to call it. Though so far you've never felt a cash crunch, right now you'll have money to burn. And that's a monthly trend. I'm reminded of that Rod Stewart number *'Some Guys Have All the Luck*!'

6 June: Last Quarter in Pisces

Your dreams, hopes, ambitions may be about to be realized now. Definitely a wish-fulfilment, particularly in love, though work comes a close second. It's time to devote energy to money matters on a large scale, not personal finances. I mean loans, joint funds, stocks and shares so that it's mega bucks for your work or business that you have to concentrate on now. Don't neglect documents, drafts, leases.

13 June: New Moon in Gemini

You as a parent, or you as a child – that's the emphasis this period. You'll have duties to perform in both roles. Family gatherings and get-togethers will have you a willing and happy participant. And you'll also be making more than successful moves at work as well. Another fine period for you, Taureans.

20 June: First Quarter in Virgo

It's time to relax a bit, slacken your speed and come to a gentle halt. You'll see the definite and promising results of your business activities and hard work in family matters. It's not good to let go totally, since there can be the danger of sliding back, so it's necessary not to be too easy-going.

28 June: Full Moon in Capricorn

You'll have to keep a firm grip on yourself so that you don't feel bored and restless or even lazy and slothful. It's time to reach out, even across the world if necessary, to people and places. Please do understand the significance of this oft-repeated phrase of mine. One reaches out to them in totally different ways, and different skills and attitudes are needed.

6 July: Last Quarter in Aries

It would almost seem that you took my advice of last period to heart. And the results are truly spectacular in terms of sharing, togetherness and warmth, not only in family ties but in all the relationships that make up the fabric of life. You'll be able to understand the hopes as well as the problems, and help very genuinely for both. It helps you assess your own self and realize your own potential – both at work and in relationships.

13 July: New Moon in Cancer

As a continuation of last period, in this realization of potential you will also be able to assess where exactly there is room for improvement. And there always is, isn't there? Anyway, clothes, make-up, hairdo, physique, computer skills, even learning to cook, you turn your mind to them all. And do a good job of it, in the bargain. Especially in the sphere of the arts, creative pursuits.

19 July: First Quarter in Libra

The assessments I've been mentioning in the last period are now focused on the home and family, the care of relatives and parents, even family resources and funds. You will look for ways and means (means, always important!) to improve them and add to the comfort, security and lifestyle of your loved ones. Wonderful.

27 July: Full Moon in Aquarius

Romance, recreation, the love of family, friends and that special someone – all warm the cockles of your heart. It's also a spectacularly lucky time for money matters, investments and even sudden, unexpected gains. This is particularly true for those in the media, the performing arts, publicity and those professions that are in the public eye. Ganesha is kind to you.

4 August: Last Quarter in Taurus

Both spiritualism and an increased libido are in store for you. You want pleasure both in this world (passion, sex, material satisfaction) and the next, for your soul. It's something that will also be reflected in your handling of finances, at which you will display a brilliance that will make you surprise yourself. Some health problems may happen but not major ones.

11 August: New Moon in Leo

A period not only of hectic activity but of heavy spending too. You will be loaded with responsibility and will rise to the occasion in every way – time, energy, funds. Some hassles over land, ancestral or new property will have to be dealt with, and paid for too. Relatives too could make demands on you in all the ways possible. A demanding period, all round.

18 August: First Quarter in Scorpio

In your own birth sign many things will work for you and all the concerns that were weighing you during the last period will see you finding brilliant solutions. And, you have time to ease off, to actually go out and grab at life itself, have a real ball, enjoy yourself at social gatherings and parties, even splurge on new decor for the home. You're certainly happier now.

26 August: Full Moon in Pisces

You will lay the foundations for great improvement in the quality of family life. It may take the form of wise investments, renovation or extension of your home, a new car, or perhaps just a new attitude. And all this despite a certain disillusionment, world-weariness or just a restless phase that you personally undergo. It's because you have learnt to exercise a degree of self-discipline and make sacrifices to attain a higher self. Once again, a long-term trend.

3 September: Last Quarter in Gemini

You're back with a bang to the two Fs of fun and family, not necessarily in that order. It's certain that the social whirligig will be important in this period, but so also loved ones, extended family, and work as an extension of yourself. It's action time on all three fronts, truly speaking. Finding the energy to cope may make too many demands. Health care is a must, so also dealing with stress.

9 September: New Moon in Virgo

You are keenly aware of less privileged people, and you care for the elderly, mentally challenged, the poor and the homeless. The reason could be the spiritual awakening and religious insights that you are now experiencing. They will draw you like a moth to a candle but with much happier results.

16 September: First Quarter in Sagittarius

Your new outlook and attitude will now be reflected in your success at channelling your creative talents. A wonderful time for those working with children or young people, or if you're one yourself. Perhaps you may experience the rebelliousness of youth too. Take care that you don't wind up as a 'rebel without a cause'.

25 September: Full Moon in Aries

A heavy workload, but with it, great easing off in terms of money. That's likely to be the trend for the next few weeks. You get the rewards and recognition – even in cash terms – that you have striven for, for so long. And richly deserved, despite your bad moments.

2 October: Last Quarter in Cancer

You'll have a lot on your plate right now. New projects and procedures at office, family and dependents to cater for too. Financial hurdles and problems will be overcome with ease, and that will be a great relief. Your own efficiency and skill will be responsible but it helps you doubly because others will be willing and cooperative, especially at the workplace.

9 October: New Moon in Libra

The successful carrying out of plans and projects over the last weeks now gives you a mighty boost in terms of poise and self-confidence. You will think positive and be determined to go out and win. This will apply to both work and money. I'm sure I don't have to spell it out further. At least, in your present state of mind!

16 October: First Quarter in Capricorn

Home improvement. Not the wackily funny TV serial, but your major concern this week. All kind of gadgets for the home, from the utilitarian to the openly luxurious like jacuzzis and a piano (if so interested) will be acquired. It's part of your search for a better, happier, more fulfilled life. You are willing to make that little extra effort, the final push that will get you where you want to be.

24 October: Full Moon in Taurus

Once again, your interest in the more distant horizons of the occult, tantra and mantra, the world of extrasensory perception (ESP) and psychism will dominate your mind, even though you will continue to perform well, both at home and in the office. Even more will you concern yourself with karma, life after death, the cycle of rebirth.

31 October: Last Quarter in Leo

There will be far less stress and strain in your life during this period. In fact, not just rest and relaxation but lots of recreation make up the three Rs for you. You still have the time and inclination to deal with the funds, loans, finances and investments theme I spoke of. Also, much better health – mentally and physically.

7 November: New Moon in Scorpio

There is a deep contentment, an inner calm prevailing in your mind, and therefore, in your life as well. You'll take the minor pinpricks of daily living well in your stride. Closeness and togetherness, sharing and warmth in all your personal equations, but most specially with your spouse/partner add to this.

15 November: First Quarter in Aquarius

It's time for close bonding with your children, but also with extended family, kin, even neighbours. You're in a helpful mood, willing to sort out others' problems. You will also be considering new projects for work and business and are ready to a) take risks for future gain and b) make extra effort at work to create better opportunities for yourself.

23 November: Full Moon in Gemini

Realizing that money has tremendous power in the world you will go all out and concentrate on all kinds of fund-raising and financial activities. That is the focus in this period. Income generation will strike you as the best means to a better life. And you're not too far wrong. It's necessary to oil the wheels of life.

30 November: Last Quarter in Virgo

How others see you, deal with you, compete with you, will be the focus now. A time for public relations, your image in the eyes of others, even open rivalry but not enmity is what you need to concentrate on. Family unity will be important. Also, family/funds/loans/investments.

7 December: New Moon in Sagittarius

Infotech. One word could easily sum up the whole gamut of communication, contacts, email and net surfing that make up your main pursuits during this period. Also, strongly emphasized will be long-distance travel, distant and foreign connections, foreign trade, export–import.

15 December: First Quarter in Pisces

You will need to work in a team both at work and within the family, presenting a solid front to the world. Long-range communication will even influence the vacation you might take, or the recreation and fun that you plan to embark on. A sense of discipline and decorum will be necessary when handling colleagues and family.

22 December: Full Moon in Cancer

The sense of adventure, the spirit of daring, that has been at the back of all your activities during the last period will find you doing brilliantly in creative and artistic fields once again. At computers and information technology, even higher education and research. But in money matters, and in family relations it will have to be kept firmly in touch.

29 December: Last Quarter in Libra

You're on a total high, not induced by drugs/strong spirits, but your own confidence and sense of self-worth. That has been the gift of the millennium for you. And I can assure you, it will yield spectacular results. Your confidence will be coupled with a willingness not only to learn, but to work hard, to strive, to struggle.

GEMINI

22 May–22 June

Geminis are kings of contacts and communication. They reach out to people and places everywhere, including the Milky Way and the immense galaxies and spaces. That's their speciality.

- **Colours:** Blue, yellow, yellow-orange
- **Colours that promotes love, romance and social harmony:** Sky blue
- **Colours that promote earning power:** Grey, silver
- **Gems:** Agate, aquamarine
- **Metal:** Quicksilver
- **Scents:** Lavender, lilac, lily of the valley
- **Quality:** Mutability (= flexibility)
- **Quality most needed for balance:** Thought that is deep rather than superficial
- **Strongest virtues:** Great communication skills, quickness and agility of thought, ability to learn quickly
- **Deepest need:** Communication

- **Characteristics to avoid:** Gossiping, hurting others with harsh speech, superficiality, using words to mislead or misinform

- **Day:** Wednesday

- **Number:** Five

- **Flowers:** Lavender, blue violet, lily of the valley

- **Trees:** Hazel, chestnut and all nut-bearing trees

- **Foods:** Nuts and all vegetables grown above the ground, except cabbage, are foods associated with Gemini, as are such herbs and spices as marjoram, caraway and aniseed

Special Message from Bejan and Nastur: You must take care of your health and finances. On the positive side, expect promotions, better work opportunities, happy relationships with pets, servants and colleagues. Care in food and regular exercise will be the secret to a happy comfortable life. I am sure you smart Geminis will get it right.

Geminis are changeable and often moody. Their symbol, the twins, means they are often at odds with themselves – the mind demanding one thing, the heart demanding the opposite. This in turn manifests as two very different people. As a Gemini's significant other, you might reach a point where you wonder which twin you are with.

JUPITER

For you intelligent Geminis I have worked out a threefold plan. The first plan will be about the focus of Jupiter in your sixth angle. This focus will be on colleagues and servants, health, food, shelter and all matters related to the necessaries of life. Except earlier job opportunities and services including even freelancing or doing handy jobs as they say or just supervising on workers will be of immense importance and purpose. Also, relatives and friends who rely upon you, pets, in fact all animals will help to shape your destiny to a great extent.

The second part of the plan is about finding your own self. By helping others, taking care of your health, innovating new systems of work, making work sound like fun and joy and being consistent and steady on the work level you will achieve much. You Geminis are brilliant but fickle, ever-changing and easily bored. That will not do now.

Lastly, please do not take matters lightly but accept your responsibility willingly and happily. Do not be sarcastic and argue over petty matters. Have a broad mind and vast mental horizon. Sometimes you Geminis lose confidence and become defensive. Therefore, I am assuring you again and again to not only overcome all obstacles but also do great and grand work.

SATURN

The two main planets I take are Jupiter and Saturn. Saturn will be in your eighth angle from 21 December 2017 to 22 March 2020. To put it simply, the eighth angle stands for taxes, loans, joint finance, inheritance, legacy, lottery, public funds and trusts, and handling very specially the funds and money of others, accidents, rebirth, great spiritual powers, tantra and mantra. But the real contradiction is that the eighth house stands for very good and noble deeds, as well as evil deeds like rape, murder, loot, arson, blackmail. You Geminis are very intelligent, exceptionally sharp. This intelligence can be used both ways. Luckily in 2018, Saturn in your eighth house and Jupiter in your sixth house are in a very fine and powerful position astrologically. Therefore, you will get both honey and money. The possible months for it are January, March, May, July (specially), September, November. Just for your information I am giving you the other features connected with the eighth house: marital status of a woman, longevity, death, obstacle, disgrace, defeat, misery, loss of memory, killing a living being, capital punishment, nature of death, place of death, wickedness, father's indebtedness, deviation from expected norms, frightful place, difficult route, crevices, finding faults, humiliation, wife's wealth, sudden unexpected gains, hidden talents, spiritual pursuits and attainments, son of an elder sister.

Obviously, all of these cannot happen. But you Geminis are very curious and therefore very specially for you I am exerting a little more and giving you all the possible information. I always take into very active consideration the outer planets, Pluto, Neptune and Uranus.

URANUS

Uranus is the planet of revolution and evolution. Therefore, you will make strange friends and acquaintances. Eccentric and intelligent people could form a group for you. The strange and mysterious effects of Uranus may be felt in February, June, August, October and December.

NEPTUNE

In 2018, Neptune remains in your angle of profession, business, parents, in-laws, prestige and power. Neptune is also superbly placed with Saturn and Pluto. Therefore, funds for any type of work or entertainment or marriage or films or events should be available. I have just invented a special phrase for you. The great car Rolls Royce also rolls on money. Let me put it all in a different way. The real year for starting an enterprise or expanding a business or having a wish-fulfilment in life is 2018. The real spin-off will be in 2019.

PLUTO

Pluto holds hands with Saturn in your eighth angle. I never command and give orders. I believe in 'Live and let live'. But if you believe in God or Mother Nature you should most certainly worship your chosen energy and power in 2018 carefully. It helps. It will protect you against evil vibrations and help you in doing good deeds. I repeat that this is only my humble suggestion. You are welcome to your own beliefs and opinions. Just for your information I am pointing out that the holy days of prayers are Fridays, Saturdays and Thursdays.

MERCURY

I am sure most of you know that your main planet is Mercury. Mercury is the communication and contacts expert of the entire zodiac. We can conquer the whole world by messages and news and views. We know all about mobile, iPad, tablets, Internet and so on. Mercury will be in your own sign from 30 May to 12 June 2018. It will work wonders for you again from 1 to 17 February, 29 June to 5 September, 22 September to 9 October, 12 December to 4 January 2019, 9 January to 24 February 2019. Again, royally favourable from 27 June to 18 July, 14 September to 2 October 2019. And again from 9 December to 28

December. It will be easier for you to get your work done speedily and happily during the periods mentioned above. I want you to use it wisely and well, so that you and all your friends get the most out of it. But please remember that I am not God and astrology at best is only a guideline. Confidence is half the battle and astrology the other half. Perhaps the colours yellow, lemon, white can be both lucky and joyous for you Geminis.

MONTHLY ROUND-UPS

January: Money, honey, riches, beautification, augmentation of income, good food, jewellery; **February:** Research, contacts, communication, correspondence, brothers, sisters, relatives; **March:** Home, house, property, renovation, decoration, alteration; **April:** Love, romance, children, relationships, hobbies, sports; **May:** Health, pets, servants, job, hygiene, colleagues; **June:** Love, marriage, divorce, journeys, reaching out to people, also separations and lawsuits; **July:** Joint finances, funds, loans, legacy, family issues and problems; **August:** Sweet-and-sour relationships, publicity, conferences and meets, inspirational and intuitive moves and manoeuvres; **September:** Prestige, status, power struggle, perks, new ventures and means of communication; **October:** Socializing, group activities, marriage, love affair, happiness, laughter, the goodies of life; **November:** Secret activities, health expenses, visits to hospitals, welfare centres, medical check-ups; **December:** Fulfilment, happiness, money, marriage, confidence.

HAPPINESS QUOTA: 78 per cent

WEEKLY REVIEW (BY PHASES OF THE MOON)

2 January: Full Moon in Cancer

It's a start that is not at all flashy, yet there is an upsurge in certain spheres. All things related to money – funds, joint finance, the buying/selling/renting/leasing of property or house, even travel and documentation. A wide range to choose from. You'll have to be business-like and practical, and temporarily shelve both family matters and merrymaking.

8 January: Last Quarter in Libra

There will be a fair amount of buying and selling of property, goods, even documents and papers that will form part of your work. Other than that, those in publicity-related fields too will be more than busy, but now domestic matters will jostle for space in your mind. Travel too, or even a shift to another place for work, or perhaps for study and research, is very likely.

17 January: New Moon in Capricorn

It's more of the same, i.e., the focus will be more on work than anything else but now is the time to put your marvellous ability to get on with people, to empathize, communicate to good use. You might even make a career of it – social work, helplines, solace to the challenged, or just a 'chat show'. All of these will yield both pleasure, profit, interest. And sustained interest is something that you can be low on.

24 January: First Quarter in Taurus

Work finally takes a back seat as you sing '*I want to break free*' into the arms of a lover, a romantic affair, or soul vibes with your mate/partner. It's a time when creativity is at white heat for you. Hobbies, the arts, music will attract you to at least appreciate and enjoy, if not perform and excel at. Homemaking skills will also find you at your best.

31 January: Full Moon in Leo

The twin themes of finance and family will continue to dominate as a trend for February, but there are higher aspirations in the picture as well. These could take the form of travel, distant connections (I mean to far-off places), advanced study and research, opportunities to make a lot of money very fast. Ganesha says, no rash moves please, Geminis.

7 February: Last Quarter in Scorpio

The tinkle of money in the coffers is sweet music to anyone's ears. Even mine. For you, Geminis, it's a made-to-order situation for finances, deals, carefully made speculation. You may be flush with funds but going on a shopping binge, as you'd like to do, should be weighed against putting by for a rainy day. Creativity, higher study, children are all highlighted too.

15 February: New Moon in Aquarius

The daredevilry and rashness of your sign comes to the fore. Wild gambles, a killing on the stock market, dangerous sports like Grand Prix or Formula One racing – you're truly flirting with life and death. The only advice Ganesha bids me to give you is check your goals, your temper, and your spending. This whole forecast applies to love and romance too. You might wind up being involved with the wrong person.

23 February: First Quarter in Gemini

It's as if you've been feeling your oats last week, and will now meekly accept the bridle. Both work pressures and home responsibilities find you coping not just willingly but almost happily, with not a snort of protest. It makes for greater harmony at home and better performance at work.

2 March: Full Moon in Virgo

Family and the neighbourhood, community affairs will be the focus this quarter, and more or less right through the month. It will also see the successful winding up of some business matters which have been very long delayed. It's a time for ties also, both personal and professional, and most importantly, for religion and prayer, philosophy and meditation. The spiritual aspect of your nature will, in fact, influence the predominant theme of home, family, relationships.

9 March: Last Quarter in Sagittarius

It's the quarter of your own birth sign, and all that you do, feel and think is bound to be specially charged, strengthened, fortified. And now your home is your castle, your bastion against a cruel and demanding world, and your family and loved ones, your raison d'être. No more chafing at the bit when responsibilities on the domestic front have to be fulfilled, or there's extra work involved.

17 March: New Moon in Pisces

It's travel, trips, ties – the three Ts going to form the total of communication, whether physical or emotional. It's definitely people and places for you. If you can't make up your mind about important decisions, delay them. A more favourable time will soon come. Expenses will go through the roof, but you'll have to try to keep from overspending on business, or there could be big trouble.

24 March: First Quarter in Cancer

Your prestige, standing in the family circle and society will probably be at an all-time high but there will also be fairly heavy responsibilities. You will have earned the popularity that you enjoy. Also important will be care of pets, dependents, the elderly. Both friends and family not only support you but will also actively participate in all your activities.

31 March: Full Moon in Libra

Determination and sheer gutsy hard work, even a kind of ruthlessness in chasing goals and targets that are beneficial to you, that's the ticket. At the same time, you have to party, wine and dine, dance and socialize. It may be that the socializing is a means to the same end – self-advancement. But that is the theme for the whole month.

8 April: Last Quarter in Capricorn

The determined efforts of last week will begin to show results right now. Perks/promotions/popularity/prestige/pelf – all the five Ps come to you but as a result of the sixth P of personal endeavour. It's your own purposeful work that has made it happen. And the other P of personal relationships will be equally wonderful, especially in terms of family reunions and bonds, special closeness to loved ones.

16 April: New Moon in Aries

The effect will be felt in the sphere of information technology and computers, metaphysics, cybernetics – all those esoteric new fields that dazzle old fogeys like me. It may give an added edge to your work now and added income to you. Thus, TV, the arts, the print media will be the fields that are greatly successful. It's not a time to let yourself become too cocksure. Read the fine print in contracts and documents and be careful not to lose them while travelling. Follow this hunch of mine!

22 April: First Quarter in Leo

Once again, you will be single-minded, strong-minded and focused. And that's saying a lot, because with the essential duality of the Gemini temperament, people of your sign are often vacillating, unable to make up their minds. You will realize that money is important, and accept the need to go out and earn it. Not so much for yourself as for your family, particularly your children if you have them, since you will feel that they need to be looked after specially.

30 April: Full Moon in Scorpio

The rewards are there now, but so also the grinding hard work that you put in to deserve these rewards. You will be truly aware of your responsibilities to your family and to society. It is a time when your conscience, the higher self, the career and provider in you will be completely awakened and will inspire you to great heights – especially intellectual and spiritual.

8 May: Last Quarter in Aquarius

Health problems may be more than likely. Read the last

sentence just above. Of course, the non-astrological reason could be either the neglect that you are prone to, or the hard work you've been putting in. You will need, and get the support of not only your friends and immediate family but of a far larger, in fact, ever-expanding social circle and network.

15 May: New Moon in Taurus

You will want to get more and more things done this week. It's as if you think you're superhuman, and are ready to perform the labours of Hercules. It might be difficult for others to cope with the demands you make on them, and there could even be resentment on their part. Patience and tact will get you far more success than finding fault. This is sage counsel from Ganesha.

22 May: First Quarter in Virgo

There will be a let-up from within you, in terms of more time and more willingness to relax, enjoy yourself, let down your guard. And this despite the still gruelling pace of work. You will be closer to your loved ones and children, will try and find time for them, even for visiting friends and neighbours. It's also a propitious time for starting up new ventures or projects.

29 May: Full Moon in Sagittarius

You are in a new avatar, much more gentle, concerned, caring and not just to loved ones and those near and dear, but to the world at large. That's a very sweeping statement, isn't it? But it's a fact that Ganesha has this as the trend for you. Warmth, bonding, tenderness, togetherness. Travel will not be too smooth.

6 June: Last Quarter in Pisces

You will make that special effort, walk that extra mile to be helpful to the sick, infirm, the young, the elderly – all the helpless ones of your circle. Pets, children, parents, even your spouse/mate, will all be cherished and cared for by you. You may even be tempted to overdo it, even financially, so that there is both a scarcity of money and maybe bad health to deal with. So, try to strike a balance, advises Ganesha.

13 June: New Moon in Gemini

It's your higher self, your other-worldly, spiritual side that dominates now. This is not to say that you abandon the world and go off to the forests on sanyas. Far from it. Family and loved ones find you warm and affectionately caring, but this will be one aspect. Personally, you're after a different kind of fulfilment and march to a different drummer.

20 June: First Quarter in Virgo

A complicated period. There will be some legal wrangles that could be bitterly fought before they are concluded. At the same time, great closeness and pleasure in material ties. Also at the same time, your research/further study/crash course/communication skills require your full concentration. Family, funds and resources will have to be looked after and made safe from risk.

28 June: Full Moon in Capricorn

The new trend will have money and finance as the main theme, but in terms of long-term financial security and both planning ahead and putting by, investing sensibly. At the same time, the theme of personal growth, mental vision, intellectual attainments, that was there in May, now becomes much stronger, and will remain so for some time. Children's problems may cause worries and tension.

6 July: Last Quarter in Aries

You seem to have finally found the answer how to balance family commitments and responsibilities and your own moneymaking abilities. With harmony restored in your mind, your thoughts turn to love and romance – ready to flirt, dally, make amorous advances! In addition, there could be a brainwave about a lucrative new line of work.

13 July: New Moon in Cancer

You are in a rather rash frame of mind, impatient of all snags and delays and are hankering for quick results. It doesn't always happen that way, my friends. There is a time required for every process, and do remember that old saying, 'Haste makes waste.' There could be more danger of losing all that you've achieved. And I mean this not only in 'money' terms, but personally as well.

19 July: First Quarter in Libra

Once again, your career and work will be strongly focused, but there is a change in that you will continue to balance it with home and family and your real self and try to attain harmony between them all. Finances will be important too, but more for family needs than anything else. You, therefore, try to reorient your ambitions and further try to include your own personal religious beliefs.

27 July: Full Moon in Aquarius

Your health is never your strong point, Geminis, and you have been having a lot of stress and could have been listless, tired, run down. You will experience, in this new moon, a major upswing and raised energy levels and resistance and stamina! Equally pleasing will be the upward graph in terms of money, perks, gifts, bonus, lucky investments. The money's really good now. In personal relationships, there could be disappointments, problems.

4 August: Last Quarter in Taurus

Travel – actual, and also of the spirit – brings gain and also a growth, a development in your personality. Your attitudes will be gentler, less egocentric, more humane and loving. Personal relationships touch heaven right now. Therefore, you will be content and have your sights firmly fixed on the way you envisage your future.

11 August: New Moon in Leo

Relationships. One word sumps it up totally – children, romantic involvements, parents, in-laws, siblings, relatives. You may get hurt due to some disputes in the family, but lawsuits and legal issues will be resolved easily and in your favour. The other vitally important feature will be the three Cs – contacts, correspondence, communication – which need to be dealt with sensibly and judiciously.

18 August: First Quarter in Scorpio

After being totally involved with family and extended family, it's now time to look out for yourself and your own ambitions. Domestic and social issues will proceed smoothly, thankfully, so that you can take action for your own interests and benefit. The media, trade, creative arts, even craft-related business, foreign trade, are all favoured and will yield profit. Go for it!

26 August: Full Moon in Pisces

A fresh, new start is what life is all about, for you Geminis. Projects, deals, interests that were in the pipeline, will now get activated, new friendships and alliances will be formed. You will visit excitingly different places, follow new leisure activities, break out of the old and stale mould into a new, very exhilarating sphere.

3 September: Last Quarter in Gemini

The monthly trend which set in last week of soaring 'Higher and still higher' for you, like Shelley's skylark, continues. There is, if anything, an add-on. You will not just impress but totally overpower everyone around by the sheer force and charm you radiate. Recognition, awards and rewards, praise and glory are a foregone conclusion. Ganesha is generous.

9 September: New Moon in Virgo

The phase extends to this quarter too. You are totally brilliant and impressive at work, to the utter amazement of your totally bemused watchers. I know I love to exaggerate, but this time it's not an exaggeration at all. Just plain, hard fact. Promotions, popularity, perks, prestige, personal interaction and parents.

16 September: First Quarter in Sagittarius

The frenzied joy, achievements, the glory and the applause finally die down. Your mind and spirit are calm, contented, and you're easy to live with yourself. You are grateful, relaxed, and have realized that you can tap your own innate resources for peace, harmony and joy of the soul, and have come well on the way to mastering the art of living, both the pun and otherwise.

25 September: Full Moon in Aries

Having achieved tangible, visible goals that are appreciated in the material world, your quest is now for higher ones. Peace and being true to yourself and to those you care for, loving and being loved. It's a fine way to be, but with typical Gemini rashness, don't ever think this can last forever without your continued striving to make it happen.

2 October: Last Quarter in Cancer

It's functioning in a group, even if it's through a website, that is your special forte now. And the outcome will be wonderful in terms of success. There will be traffic snarl ups on this journey, and challenges too, but you sail through. Nobody and nothing can stop you when you're in search of your own personal space, but the going could get rough in terms of health.

9 October: New Moon in Libra

Yourself, yourself as the centre of a group, and now yourself in the centre of home and family. The trend has a line of progression in it. Your responsibilities and family will make demands on your time and attention that you cannot deny. So too will your career. It's up to you to balance them both well and happily.

16 October: First Quarter in Capricorn

You will not only realize your own true potential capabilities and skills but also all the doubts and questions about your actions, and their outcome, will now melt away. You will be stronger, more self-reliant even though that can't be said about your actual health. I'm talking now of other strengths: a) career/business/vocation and b) spirituality/religion/faith.

24 October: Full Moon in Taurus

You've not only worked hard but sincerely, devoted to the highest objectives of others before self. Time to relax, unwind, pick out some goodies from the bag of life. These could be entertaining and entertainment, parties, socializing, holidays and vacations, or even all of them, if you have managed to grab a fistful! This is the trend for the month.

31 October: Last Quarter in Leo

You will realize that discretion and care are essential if you want to put financial troubles behind you and be totally self-sufficient and independent in money matters. You may even want to set up an independent, home-based business/office for this. Also, equally important for you will be your personal journeys of faith, tantra, mantra, prayer and worship. I'm not talking of pilgrimages or visits to holy places so much as meditation, spiritualism as you try to get closer to realization of God.

7 November: New Moon in Scorpio

A kind of hankering for being alone, like Christ wandering in the desert, will possess you. You may even be full of doubts, despair and questions. These mood swings are part of the Gemini psyche and you feel you require a change of location or scene to make you feel better. Travel or weekend trips are likely. So also, working for the community concerns about global environment, for society and for human welfare.

15 November: First Quarter in Aquarius

There will not only be a total, but very visible and definite change in your attitude after the new moon. Your self-doubts, worries may not disappear but they will certainly be set at rest, and the good thing is that the change comes from within. Family and work demands will be tackled with determination and tact, so that you get quick and pleasing results.

23 November: Full Moon in Gemini

In this new mood of squaring up to reality, you will focus firmly on your family, loved ones and friends, and be prepared to go all out for them. Your social and philanthropic concerns, work for charity, and larger causes too. You will have the insight and perception to be able to foresee trends for the future and adjust your own activities accordingly.

30 November: Last Quarter in Virgo

You're ready for action, if it means starting the process of change. But you realize the need to do so gradually, not totally upset the apple cart. You will also realize that a certain steadiness helps relationships and will try hard to maintain it. Money will be important in terms of planning budgets for home and office.

7 December: New Moon in Sagittarius

Both your career and your social life show an upward slant, like the last few overs shown on a graph in a One-day cricket match. You will be able to combine work and recreation, home affairs and work demands, in short, business and pleasure. You will be making, or at least weighing up, decisions that could affect your future and your family.

15 December: First Quarter in Pisces

A tremendously busy, even fraught, phase starts. And you'll be busy in your every possible way, work, socializing, family affairs and functions, even some secret negotiations and/or politics, if that way inclined. In fact, you'll have to make a conscious effort to relax and rest or there could be a total burnout. Financial jugglery or at least rethinking of it will also be part of this activity, as you think of new ways, to add to your income, balance the budget, and save for the future.

22 December: Full Moon in Cancer

Major opportunities for gain started coming your way from the end of October. Finances will be good – legacies, inheritances, gifts and windfalls! Great joy in family life, in social interaction. The year ends with a joyous note, with perhaps a stroke of luck too, in the last few days of the years, through the great power of Ganesha.

29 December: Last Quarter in Libra

Bonds, ties, partnerships, relationships, links – that is what Ganesha sees for you as the old year gives rise to the new. Communication is the name of the game – it may range from email, net surfing, to just a platonic kiss on the cheek. I'm an inveterate romantic at heart, so I think I'd prefer the kiss to being told 'You've got mail'. And I'm telling you I'm not kidding too much.

CANCER
❦

23 June–22 July

'It is hard to imagine what the world would be like without the geometry of Euclid, the philosophy of Pythagoras, the logic and literature of Aristotle and the fables of Aesop, not forgetting the Olympic games with their spirit of peace and brotherhood. Words such as philanthropy, harmony, music, architecture and ecology that we use so often today are derived from Greek.'

I am very sure that the above paragraph has motivated and inspired you. You Cancerians are intuitive and psychic; therefore you must have felt in your bones and marrow that the goodies of life are coming your way.

- **Element:** Water

- **Ruling planet:** Moon

- **Colours:** White, opal, iridescent silvery hues, smoky grey, sea green and blue

- **Colours that promote love, romance, and social harmony:** Black, indigo

- **Colours that promote earning power:** Gold, orange.

- **Gems:** Moonstone, pearl

- **Metal:** Silver

- **Scents:** Jasmine, sandalwood

- **Quality:** Cardinal (=activity)

- **Quality most needed for balance:** Mood control

- **Strongest virtues:** Emotional sensitivity, tenacity, the urge to nurture

- **Deepest need:** A harmonious home and family life

- **Characteristics to avoid:** Oversensitivity, negative moods

- **Best day of the week:** Monday

- **Body parts ruled by Cancer:** The breasts and stomach. Cancerians love to eat and have to fight obesity in later years, and also digestive ailments.

- **Cities:** Amsterdam, New York, Istanbul, Tokyo, Algiers

- **Countries:** Scotland, Holland, New Zealand and Paraguay

- **Number:** Two

- **Flowers:** White lily, acanthus, white rose, larkspur, convolvulus, water lily, all white flowers

- **Trees:** All trees, particularly those rich in sap

- **Foods:** Milk, fish, fruits and vegetables with a high water content, white and red cabbage, and herbs such as verbena and tarragon are all linked with Cancer

Special Message from Bejan and Nastur: Emotionally, Cancerians act and react in the same way the crab moves:

sideways. They avoid confrontations and usually aren't comfortable in discussing what they feel. Cancers are intuitive and sometimes psychic. Experience flows through them emotionally. They are often moody and always changeable; their interests and social circles shift constantly. Once a Cancer trusts you, however, he lets you in on his most private world. Summary: Romance and finance fuse happily for you. Health safeguards will be essential. Plenty of movement physically, mentally, emotionally, spiritually, points out Ganesha, and His is the last word.

JUPITER

'Whatever defect I have of eye, of heart, of mind, or whatever exam there is, may Brihaspati (Jupiter) remedy it. Gracious to us he, the Lord of the world' – Yajur Veda 36:2. Yes, Jupiter in Indian astrology is best known as the 'Lord of the world'. And Jupiter will be in your fifth angle from 10 October 2017 to 8 November 2018.

By Western Astrology, Jupiter has a very great influence on the sign of Cancer. It spells prosperity. When Jupiter is in the fifth angle (or the sign Cancer), it is even more powerful and beneficial. In 2018, Jupiter will be in the fifth angle.

Jupiter will unfold for you the following: Your heart will sing, '*I drink to myself and one another/And may that one another be she!*', even if you are a teetotaller. Rightly so too. Jupiter will make you attractive and charming and thus draw in your opposite number. Also, 2018 is for journeys, long-distance connections, socializing, friendship and fraternity. Yes, you will be working like a Trojan and savouring life to the maximum.

Let me begin by saying that this year will be significant for good health, confidence, prestige, status, recognition, rewards, new opportunities, travel, intuition, philosophy, spirituality and wisdom. Need more be said? Jupiter will lubricate your intellect, pep it up with all sorts of pills and goodies so to say, and will galvanize you into great action!

Love, romance, hobbies, children (starting of conception, or actual delivery of a child); exceptional creative pursuits requiring imagination and organization; the use of tantra and mantra; a possible recall of your past life or lives (you are most welcome to have your own opinion of past life or reincarnation); success in property affairs, buying and selling or just developing; new and vast outlets of entertainment and amusement, or it could be a different way or style of entertainment (example a film story, a terrific directional venture); speculation and indulgence in games of chance (example horse racing) are foretold. A word of warning, please. This is only a solar-scopic reading, not a real horoscopic one. Results and predictions are therefore not guaranteed to come correct.

SATURN

By Western astrology, Saturn will be in your seventh angle from 21 December 2017 to 22 March 2020. Let me say straight away that Saturn will blow hot and cold for you. The biggest advantage of it is that you will never have a dull moment in your life. It will be up and down and roundabout. It will be like a merry-go-round. Be sure of changes in personal and professional relationships. That is the real secret and clue to the purpose of Saturn in your seventh angle. The other noteworthy features are:

a) Connections, contacts, reaching out to people and places;

b) Journey, ceremony, legal matters;
c) Public relationships and competition, change of locale/ surrounding;
d) Collaborations and cooperation.

Ganesha dances full of jest, humour and slight mischief. In 2018, Saturn will be in a fine placing with Jupiter. Therefore, if changes are forced upon you take it in the right spirit. I know you are very sensitive, very kind, very loving, and therefore you get hurt very easily. Ganesha and Allah say, accept changes naturally and then move forward in your life. Prayers, meditations, mantras, tolerance, understanding the other person's point of view will most certainly help. If you like, you may recite the mantra, 'Shree Ram, Jay Ram, Jay Jay Ram'. Take care of lawsuits and quarrels or very petty matters. The surprising part of it all is that attainment of status and recovery of lost wealth are also very possible.

Please take 2018 and 2019 as one unit because Saturn will be in your seventh angle throughout.

MARS

Moon is the main planet for you Cancerians. But Moon changes signs every ¼ day. Therefore, I am taking the next important planet Mars for you. Mars will help you in diametrically opposite directions, namely, a) romance, hobbies, children, creative pursuits, games of chance and b) prestige, profession, work areas, promotion, profit, success. Especially important periods for it will be 1 to 20 January, 13 August to 10 September and 16 November to 31 December 2018. July, your birth month, will show the way to happiness and health.

URANUS

Uranus will be responsible for changes in the nature and scope of your work. Even if you are ninety years old, your brain cells will jiggle and jump and you will be able to work efficiently. Evidently this should make you feel very confident. As you all know, confidence is certainly the sister, if not the mother, of success. Finally, I say very sincerely and humbly, 'May Ganga Maiya go with you emotional, sensitive, kind, nervous, slightly insecure Cancerians.'

NEPTUNE

Neptune is your best bet. How and why? Neptune will be in your ninth angle of inspiration, imagination, psychic powers, religion, spirituality and perhaps glimpses of God or nature or whatever else you believe in. Secondly, Neptune rules over the sea. The element of you Cancerians is water. Therefore, once again Neptune will give you an insight into the nature of all things above including creation itself. Time to invent, time to discover, time for a bit of romance, time for great fun, time for making merry and if you want you can also marry. Choice is yours. In short, an excellent mix of joy and sorrow awaits you.

PLUTO

Pluto embraces Saturn in your seventh angle. Result? Exciting adventure in all areas of human contacts, attachments and affairs. It means you will be lively and possibly dancing on your toes with joy and sorrow both. Let me now make a confession. I am also a Cancerian and this will probably apply to me. Journeys and ceremonies are very probable. My advice to you once again is, let life take its own force and go with the flow. Your circle of friends will increase and therefore your orbit of influence will be as wide as the sky itself.

MONTHLY ROUND-UPS:

January: Power, pelf, perks, promotion, prosperity; **February**: Finances and family; **March**: Contacts and joy; **April**: Property, parents, renovation/decoration, parents, in-laws; **May**: Joy, creativity, children, hobbies, you make news and win others over; **June**: Work, funds, employment, health and medical check-up, servants, subordinates; **July**: Marriage, ties, love, collaborations, romance, meeting and reaching out to people and places; **August**: Health, funds, vitality, tantra and mantra, change of locale, moving; **September**: Journeys, publicity, ceremonies, collaborations, functions, rites and religion; **October**: Stepping up on efficiency, work, status, prestige, taking care of parents, elders; **November**: Help, socializing, friendship, fraternity, camaraderie; **December**: Expenses, losses, spirituality, helping others, charity, long-distance connections.

HAPPINESS QUOTA: 83 per cent

WEEKLY REVIEW (BY PHASES OF THE MOON)

2 January: Full Moon in Cancer

You start the year in a true sunburst of glory – you have the Midas touch in all you undertake, all you do! Home and domestic issues are quiet and composed but work will be wonderfully rewarding and satisfying. It is the money angle, though that spells out rewards, satisfaction, success. Bonds, securities, joint finance, perhaps even golden handshakes, as you move on to something different, something better.

8 January: Last Quarter in Libra

True creativity, intellectual genius, even brilliance, joy and success in relationships. What a trend! You have all the right skills as well as the right ideas. Glamour, inspiration, chutzpah give you achievements and success in all your undertakings and with the people who matter most to you. And here I'm talking of the entirely personal relationships and bonds that make it all worthwhile!

17 January: New Moon in Capricorn

From the very first few days of the year, the going has been good, as I've pointed out. It is especially good now in terms of both personal and professional growth, progress, recognition. Both better health and better money make you much more dynamic. This will reflect on not only your work angle – that much is obvious – but on the quality and tone of your relationships, your interaction with people in general and with your special people.

24 January: First Quarter in Taurus

More and more is what Ganesha has decided to give you. He seems to be showing us what true generosity is all about. There is good health, marvellous romance, joy in relationships, falling in love all over again. Some diehard romantics like me, in fact, never fall out of it. It's good to be in love with life – keeps one young at heart! Position and status, power, prestige, recognition all register tremendous gains too.

31 January: Full Moon in Leo

The year 2018 started very well for you and has continued to be good. Anyone might be justified in thinking it won't last, but it does! You get more good things and they are the type to last. There is a renewal of faith, an avowal of spiritual leanings, prayer, reverence for the Supreme Being. Even the philosophical, the metaphysical, the life one leads (?) after death, will exercise and brighten your mind.

7 February: Last Quarter in Scorpio

Two trends for this month instead of one predominant theme. On the one hand, you will seek solitude to promote meditation, contemplation, your inner health. This will be the direct offshoot of last week's spirituality. On the other hand, you relate so well to people, and are so energetic, confident, successful that the angle of entertainment, hospitality, social intercourse will be equally energized.

15 February: New Moon in Aquarius

You will be closer than ever to your family, your loved ones and above all, to your own self, your identity, your individuality. Your heritage and ancestry, your roots will be more important than ever. You'll seek to fix them more firmly in your own consciousness and awareness. All this will happen despite a good deal of travel. It could, of course, even be because of it.

23 February: First Quarter in Gemini

Dreams are coming true – with the full moon phase in your own sign. Long-cherished hopes, ambitions, wishes will now become concrete realities. A sense of achievement is a fine way to feel. Ganesha gives it to you now, but he adds on a warning against pushing too hard and expecting too much from others.

2 March: Full Moon in Virgo

You are not workaholic the way you can often be. But they have great focus, determination, single-mindedness. In this phase, it is these qualities that will direct you to the work arena. Please note the word 'arena' – where gladiators went out to win in combats to the thunderous applause of spectators. You will also attach problems, disputes, perhaps even some of them pertaining to family property.

9 March: Last Quarter in Sagittarius

You will be brilliant and successful – impressively so – in your professional life/career/job. Politicians would kill to have the kind of dream run you've been having since the start of 2018. And Ganesha tells me that it will continue for some months more. All this, as I've said earlier, reflects gloriously and beautifully on your family life, on your love/ marriage interactions, on your dealings with both parents and children.

17 March: New Moon in Pisces

You feel that you must give your best, perhaps your all to the family you hold so dear. Particularly so for your spouse/ partner/lover, with whom there are joys, the perennial delights that come from the union of both flesh and soul. This is not an exaggeration – I'm just trying to describe how good it will all be!

24 March: First Quarter in Cancer

Marvellous but hectic activity now. It's so good that you wouldn't have it any other way. And the activity will centre around money and honey (love) – my favourite phrase. Both will be brilliantly satisfying and you'll be thinking of all possible ways to keep it that way. You're on to so many good things that only a fool would let them go. And a fool you're not.

31 March: Full Moon in Libra

Recreation, wining and dining, being entertained, extending hospitality – having a rare good old time is what I see you doing now. Joy that is boundless and deep comes to you in the love/marriage angle. There could be both love and marriage happening now too. Sometimes love preoccupies a person so that friendship gets excluded.

8 April: Last Quarter in Capricorn

You may not want to, but you'll still have to focus very strongly on the finances now. You have to make some bold moves and decisions, the right choices according to your own conviction of where money and security lie. It won't be a time for boldness, though, on the family scene. There could be disputes and problems to sort out, feelings of real or imagined neglect to soothe, some gestures of conciliation to be made.

16 April: New Moon in Aries

You will consciously slow down the pace at which you're living and make an effort to take things easy. Maybe the allegations of neglect have rankled, even if they are not true.

In fact, I should have said 'specially if they're not true'. You bring a sense of style and lots of flair to your handling of people you're close to, sparing no effort. Even though it's done with restraint, there's no holding back.

22 April: First Quarter in Leo

Now that your personal equations are ticking over so smoothly – to the mutual satisfaction of all concerned, I must add – your public persona has to live up to the gloss and glamour. Let me assure you that it does. You are gracious, warm, humane, yet so brilliant and impressive that people are flooded by it!

30 April: Full Moon in Scorpio

No one can ever be in doubt of the fact that your approach to work is so committed that it's almost perfect! Your work angle is in focus now, and the results of your own willing, determined efforts. Your publicity will be so good that you might not believe in it. You will be genuinely helpful, sharing, sincere with your co-workers and colleagues, efficient with bosses, humane and fair with employees.

8 May: Last Quarter in Aquarius

Your expenses will be something else – they're so high. You've spent generously on all fronts; in fact, money was burning a hole in your pockets. Now you have the money to make sure that you don't let anyone down, or renege on promises, deals, payments. If you have the income to cope – and you do; Ganesha ensures it – you're willing to spend some more.

15 May: New Moon in Taurus

You will be relaxed, comfortable, at ease, easy-going. All this is especially good considering that you're now hobnobbing with the rich and famous, rubbing shoulders with the top brass, with people of distinction. You have the confidence to hold your own. It also makes it easier to continue with your devotion to family and loved ones, to older people and to those who depend on you.

22 May: First Quarter in Virgo

Skill, efficiency, single-minded concentration and of course, efficiency – these are what you get now. They're all directed to your work at which you're truly brilliant without being self-centred. It is another matter entirely that you are equally brilliant at fun, socializing, pleasurable activities.

29 May: Full Moon in Sagittarius

Something will transpire to make you take a very different line, a new modus operandi. It will be a mental shift, not an action that makes you withdraw. What is hidden, mysterious, unrevealed will appeal to you. Parapsychology, metaphysics, little-known sciences, exploration and archaeology, exploration of the mind, of genes, of cosmic truths.

6 June: Last Quarter in Pisces

If you are analytical, look back on the success and glory of the past period, you will feel thankful of course, but will also seek to analyse, search for reasons for it. You will realize now that you get your power, strength, motives – all of them – from your joy in family, domesticity, the bonds of matrimony, love, kinship.

13 June: New Moon in Gemini

Power: one word sums up the heightened awareness and activity of this phase in your own sign. Many benefits are in store for you now. You may have a wish-fulfilment, the realization of a dream. Relationships and ties, bonds and tie-ups are what matter most from the personal bonds of love and matrimony to the professional partnerships, collaborations that lead to future gain.

20 June: First Quarter in Virgo

All the power plays of the last period will show some really fast, and really glorious results. Rewards, recognition, all the parameters of success are yours once more. When I say all, I mean all. More money, more perks, more benefits add up to a fine financial angle too.

28 June: Full Moon in Capricorn

If your dreams didn't come true – or not quite the way you had envisaged – in your moon quarter, they might be clicking now. Or there could be other dreams, wishes, ambitions that take concrete shape now. Whichever way you look at it, the realization of hopes and plans should be happening now, unless there's something in your personal horoscope that makes it otherwise.

6 July: Last Quarter in Aries

True creativity – and all the fields that hinge on that, like media, infotech, the arts and literature, in particular, event and portfolio management; a vast range indeed – will be greatly favoured. People will respond to your charm and charisma, relationships will be revitalized. So also, will love.

However, what is most vital, most alive is your intensely personal, private space where not even love/spouse can enter.

13 July: New Moon in Cancer

You may find all of a sudden that there is a dynamic, diametric shift from the trends of the last period. The home, the domestic scene, will take up most of your time and attention. It's not that you won't work; it's also not that you won't play. But both work and pleasure will be coloured and influenced by family involvements.

19 July: First Quarter in Libra

You will realize that life in the fast lane is over for the time being. It's not that you're suddenly taking a break/holiday and leading a relaxed, easy-going life. There will be intense but internalized activity as you lay bare your soul, your innermost being, before your own eyes. Go in for some intensive, deep introspection, try to determine your values and future course of action.

27 July: Full Moon in Aquarius

You have decided that your family is your first priority, and this entire period is a confirmation of that belief, that conviction. In family are included siblings, cousins, older relatives, parents, in-laws. Even the fair amount of travel you engage in helps renew old ties, acquaintances, contacts. Your personal sense of worth and self-esteem will be very important in this context.

August 4: Last Quarter in Taurus

You may look back on the last period as a small interlude of peace in your hectic, schedule. All the activities that you were putting off are now back with a bang, and you're off at the same pace. You will be involved with lots of dedicated hard work, determined effort and equally deep emotional commitment, intense and vibrant love and passion and even deep sexual bondage.

11 August: New Moon in Leo

You will shine as perhaps the brightest star in the social firmament, entertaining hospitably and lavishly, being a welcome guest, partying and socializing. All this will be done with your usual panache, but perhaps this is a facade, a mask you're wearing to cover up what I spoke of in the last period. That is a deeply personal side of you that you may not want others to see.

18 August: First Quarter in Scorpio

You will be quiet, introspective, thinking of lifestyle changes, the quieter life, more placid ways and your own inner values. You realize that there must be deep-rooted and fundamental changes and are both willing and keen to make them. It's not just boredom or ennui that makes you think this way. It is a firm belief – and you wish to act on it.

26 August: Full Moon in Pisces

You may wish to withdraw from the world, but it's a moot point whether the world will let you! Not this period, at any rate, no matter how keen your desire to do so. Communication – in every possible manner, by every possible means – would sum up your activities in this period. You're brilliant as a negotiator/troubleshooter and take some wise decisions to defuse tensions too.

3 September: Last Quarter in Gemini

All the zodiac signs get activated, even stirred up, during moon phases in their own sign. It is not noticeable in the new moon phase, because that is when a trend starts for the lunar month. Achievements and gains of all kinds come to you now, as do greater efficiency, skills and expertise. It is not, says Ganesha, the time for complacency and overconfidence even if you have so much going for you.

9 September: New Moon in Virgo

A fine sense of direction and focus come to you. You know how to wear the mantle of success and which way to go in the future. In money matters too. Additionally, you are able to accept your role in life and also your responsibilities – to work, to family, and to your own self. Your personal growth and development will be important during this period.

16 September: First Quarter in Sagittarius

Both love and family angles will be pleasant, soothing, peaceful. Children and spouse in particular make for truly contented moments. There is closer bonding and oneness in both love and affection. It makes you calm, well adjusted and at peace with yourself. It also gives you an almost cosmic awareness, a deep faith and spiritual strength.

25 September: Full Moon in Aries

With the special insights of the last period, you will examine all your relationships almost under a microscope. You will also seek to put them into perspective. You redefine your own role to your parents, your children, your spouse or lover or mate. In all, you will seek to fulfil the expectations they have of you. These expectations will not be voiced by them but perceived by you.

2 October: Last Quarter in Cancer

The pressures of work never go away from you. In addition, you will feel the pressures, pulls, demands. It is still a time for success and achievements, though not as spectacular as during the first half of the year. That is the way it was for you last year too. And like last year, this year too, you find that the first half spelt out as material/worldly success and the second half, as spiritual emotional growth.

9 October: New Moon in Libra

The tensions, worries, fears and anxieties of the past period will fade away now. Ease and comfort in living, peace and calm of mind are experienced. Work/business/career will find you greatly successful. In fact, you have been successful right through but the satisfaction quotient will be much higher now. It is not just experienced professionally.

16 October: First Quarter in Capricorn

Fun, family, entertaining and finance – once again, they are all there, but on a much larger scale now. Therefore, heavier expenses are bound to happen too. Finances too will not mean family or domestic budgeting alone. There could be international transactions and transfers of funds, joint finances, deals abroad, also collaborations mergers, tie-ups.

24 October: Full Moon in Taurus

You are in a mood to solve problems, extend help, support commitment. These problems could be global or world-related, or closer to home. Your attitude will be equally sincere and caring towards both. Also, while dealing with financial matters like generating capital, dealing with loans, trusts, endowments, you take equally good care of your dependents, children, servants, in-laws.

31 October: Last Quarter in Leo

If Ganesha gave you no spare time. He must be fair and give you the energy, willpower, strength to cope. And that's just what you experience now. Love and money angles will be particularly energized. Health will be better. You'll also take better care of yourself physically. You want to be fighting fit, in appearance and turnout too.

7 November: New Moon in Scorpio

Realizing that you cannot live in splendid isolation, as you were tempted to do in the previous period, you now brush up communication skills, and public relations. New places will attract you. New friends enthuse and excite you. There is a glorious exchange of ideas, opinions, hopes and plans. Your enthusiasm, energy, joie de vivre – all register wonderful gains!

15 November: First Quarter in Aquarius

You got so much of social interaction and friendship that you will now raise it to the level of a fine art! This is no exaggeration. New friends and old, and even your rivals, competitors, enemies – you interact with them all. Only the ways will vary! Your performance at interviews, meetings, presentations, debates will be dazzling. And it's not just a performance – you are truly communicating.

23 November: Full Moon in Gemini

People and people and people. That's how important they will be for you. As I said in the last period, even rivals and competitors. You are now confident, full of energy, daring, enterprising, ready to take on everyone. You are loving, warm, caring – and busy. You will be popular, successful, very much in demand at social gatherings, functions, ceremonies.

30 November: Last Quarter in Virgo

I told you that Ganesha was pleased. Therefore, he gives you many rewards – success, power, recognition and prestige, perks and benefits. These are the tangibles. In addition, his gifts are greater intuition and perceptiveness, therefore much more kindness, tolerance, warmth, sincere caring and affection.

7 December: New Moon in Sagittarius

We talked of your spiritual gains just above. It is now that you will find them much more apparent. You will realize just how important true values and idealism have become for you. They form part of your psyche, your ethos. Your desire for excellence and achievement will still be there. Now, however, you strive for personal growth and development, for excellence in the spiritual, moral, social and personal spheres.

15 December: First Quarter in Pisces

You will not seek to exhibit or show off your personal values, idealism, even convictions. All this is bound to reflect beautifully on both your professional life/work and your personal relationships. Perhaps you are afraid it will all get dissipated or frittered away. Perhaps it is too intensely personal to be displayed. However, you will be concerned about how others see you, about the image you project.

22 December: Full Moon in Cancer

You will have that desire and the confidence to try to excel in new fields; new challenges will be faced, fresh skills acquired. You are not content to just sit back and congratulate. You want fresh new worlds to conquer. You want to prove yourself all over again – to yourself, and perhaps, to Ganesha. Perhaps you feel that where you're happiest, where things go best for you in terms of satisfaction, is at home.

29 December: Last Quarter in Libra

You will seek to address disputes, contentions regarding family/joint property; perhaps there could be family funds or even a divorce to be negotiated. What you realize now is that that is where you're needed the most. In spite of this, you are not willing to compromise one iota with your career/ professional goals and demands.

LEO

∽≫≪∽

23 July–22 August

Ganesha says different strokes for different signs. For Leos and Sagittarians the biggest is the best.

- **Element:** Fire
- **Colours:** Orange, gold, red
- **Colours that promote love, romance and social harmony:** Black, indigo, ultramarine blue
- **Colours that promote earning power:** Yellow, yellow-orange
- **Metal:** Gold
- **Quality:** Fixed (=stability)
- **Quality most needed for balance:** Humility
- **Strongest virtues:** Leadership ability, self-esteem and confidence, generosity, creativity, love of joy
- **Deepest needs:** Fun, elation, the need to shine
- **Characteristics to avoid:** Arrogance, vanity, bossiness
- **Day:** Sunday

- **Gemstone:** Ruby
- **Animals ruled by Leo:** Lion and all felines
- **Hazards:** Leo people tend to be challenging and boastful; they are also prone to being victims of slander and violence, since they are impulsive and often domineering
- **Flowers:** Sunflower, marigold, celandine, passion flower
- **Trees:** Laurel, bay tree, palm, walnut

Special Message from Bejan and Nastur: Leos have an innate dramatic sense, and life is definitely their stage. Don't ever argue to change the opinions and beliefs of a Leo. You won't succeed and the Leo will just be annoyed with you. As a fixed sign, Leos stand firm in their belief systems. They have found what works for them and don't understand why their beliefs might not work for someone else. In general, though, they are optimistic, honourable, loyal and ambitious.

Cooing and wooing, marriage, collaborations, work and rewards, mind-blowing experiences, creativity at white heat, journeys and trips and immigration, children, hobbies, entertainment, communication expertise at all levels – well, that's as exciting an adventure as you can hope to have, winks Ganesha.

JUPITER

Jupiter will be in your fourth angle from 10 October 2017 to 8 November 2018. Jupiter will focalize home, house, office, godown, warehouse, renovation and decoration, interior design, architecture, garden, orchards, hidden treasures, knowledge of geography, comforts, relatives on mother's side, agricultural produce, perfumes, clothes and milk. It will also include buying and selling of property, stores and any huge or small item which could mean very much, specially to you. I would suggest that if you like you can install a small temple or devalaya or mandir or altar in your own house or office. Why? Jupiter means great good luck in all directions.

SATURN

By Western astrology Saturn will be in your sixth angle from 21 December 2017 to 22 March 2020. We all know that work is worship. It is a cliché. But it holds true. You Leos work intelligently as well as diligently. Obviously, the result will be success. At the same time, Saturn in the sixth angle demands periodic rest, relaxation, recuperation – the three Rs. Why? Saturn is a great taskmaster. Imagine Saturn with a whip lashing you on to perform your duty, achieve your goals and targets, and take upon your shoulders all responsibilities. I know you Leos are strong and powerful. But all of us are human and need a break.

Pluto the power planet also joins Saturn in your sixth house. Therefore, it means harder work and more efficiency. The other important elements connecting with your sixth angle are those dealing with servants, pets, maternal aunt, maternal uncles, and perhaps loans, deaths and theft. The positive aspect of all this will be that Saturn in your sixth angle will be making fine placement with Jupiter in your fourth angle of house and home in 2018. That means, give your best shot in 2018 and have happy results in 2019. We all know that Sun is the main planet for you high-powered Leos. The second main planet I take will be Venus.

Love and romance is highlighted from 18 January to 10 February 2018. Journeys, ceremonies, pilgrimages from 7 to 30 March. You will find yourself fusing pleasure and profit between 25 April and 19 May. Domestic and personal affairs are highlighted between 14 June and 9 July, while the period from 7 August to 8 October is for having a ball but also being kicked about like a football. You should be sitting pretty between 1 November and 2 December, having achieved much.

I am sure you know by now that I give great importance to the outer planets Uranus, Neptune and Pluto. They are all like intercontinental missiles. In other words, they are planets which have an influence over many years.

URANUS

Uranus will help you to evolve, imagine and innovate very specially in 2019. You will be bursting with new ideas, some realistic and others totally impossible. The reason is Uranus's mighty powerful energy which often rebels and chooses a different direction. Uranus is a rocket which can zoom zap zoom up in any direction. Let me point out here that from 5 March, Uranus will be shifting to your tenth angle of profession, power and prestige. I consider it as a good sign but in the long run it will bring about changes which may be beyond your control. You Leos are not happy with changes as you are self-opinionated, stubborn, dogmatic. My advice to you is to be a little flexible and to try to flow with the current. Believe me it will be good for everybody!

NEPTUNE

Neptune will be in your eighth angle of taxes, legacies, inheritance, tantra and mantra, pension, hidden treasures, research, invention, psychic powers and even genuine spirituality. You can work from your office and/or your home and house. My only request is if you feel like it, you may take the blessings of your elders.

PLUTO

Pluto, as I have already explained, has a handshake with Saturn. Therefore, all that applies to Saturn in your sixth angle is doubly emphasized.

MONTHLY ROUND-UPS

January: Expenses, secret deals, negotiations, trips, ties; **February**: Success, projects, ventures, funds, children, creativity, good luck; **March**: Money, family promises, promotion, perks; **April**: Contacts, communication, contracts, research, import–export; **May**: Home, house, renovation, buying/selling, ill health, retirement; **June**: Fine all-round performance; you strike it lucky, and win applause; **July**: Loans, funds, joint finance, domestic matters, job, health; **August**: Love, hate, marriage, divorce, contradictory influences; **September**: Loans and funds, health and pets, religion, spirituality, rites for the living and the dead; **October**: Freedom, intuition, inspiration, publicity, long-distance connections; **November**: Work, parents, status, rivalry, prestige, tremendous pressure; **December**: Friendship, wish-fulfilment, material gains, socializing, group activities, happiness and health. You end on a positive, winning, winsome note.

HAPPINESS QUOTA: 81 per cent

WEEKLY REVIEW (BY PHASES OF THE MOON)

2 January: Full Moon in Cancer

Money matters will remain the keynote in this year. Expenses will necessarily be high, though not unexpected. The activities you undertake will demand this. You would like to care for, cherish, heal the sick, infirm, old, and the mentally sick or hurt people of society at large, not just your immediate family. And that requires money along with the large heart that you undoubtedly have.

8 January: Last Quarter in Libra

This is a wonderful kick-start for all the twelve signs for the new millennium. Along with the major thrust last week that started in terms of caring for others, you will surprise yourself with how far out on a limb you're willing to go for others, how willing you are to serve. You will now be ready to tackle whatever comes your way with gusto and determination.

17 January: New Moon in Capricorn

You will focus on all the practicalities of daily living, on your job, employment prospects, on loans or funds for projects, even a change of job if it fits in better with your larger plan for life. It may include, in addition to concern for society, equal concern for the environment, for ecology, flora and fauna, even household pets and animals.

24 January: First Quarter in Taurus

You will feel yourself put upon, as if others are imposing on you, taking you for granted. This could lead to confrontations or conflicts at work, or with your superiors over privileges and perks that you consider your due. Perhaps you'll have to stoop to conquer. It's not easy for you to play second fiddle but it may just be needed right now, and recognition of your true worth will follow.

31 January: Full Moon in Leo

I told you recognition would follow – you will see a burst of renewed self-esteem, confidence, a wonderful image of yourself, in your own eyes and those of others. You renew old friendships, make new bonds, even with siblings. In more concrete terms, there are gains, more property, more finances. A wonderful trend for the next few weeks, and don't you just love it!

7 February: Last Quarter in Scorpio

Property matters will remain at the forefront. You may either acquire, renovate or pay for upkeep. Mainly this will centre on the house and home – renovation, decoration, buying things, perhaps a new carpet/curtains/furniture/gadget. The emphasis is on personal property, not your office.

15 February: New Moon in Aquarius

All kinds of ties and partnerships are focused. Prominent will be court cases or legal matters but there will also definitely be collaborations for both work and matters of the heart. Yes, your emotions and love life, with a touch of romance for even the most diehard cynics.

23 February: First Quarter in Gemini

Your own vibrant personality, your true generosity, now gets a chance to shine through. People will be everything to you – work-based and professional interaction as well as socializing and partying till the wee hours. Gains too, in many concrete ways, including money. It will all be undone, though, if you show a lack of cooperation or too much of ego, warns Ganesha.

2 March: Full Moon in Virgo

There may be a lot of entertaining, dining out, guests and visitors to cook and cater for. I would, therefore, say that the three Fs – food, family, finances – sum it up for you as a trend for the month to come. Also, a gain in terms of spirituality, even meditation, but definitely very strong faith, and dealing in both tantra and mantra. A lot to do, both for you and for Ganesha.

9 March: Last Quarter in Sagittarius

Even more things are highlighted, now. It's all that has gone in the forecast for last week, but with the addition of new inventions, discoveries, ideas, higher study, higher questions of faith and religion. This upward spiral will also be seen in clever financial moves and investments, and last but not the least, the welfare and activities of your children.

17 March: New Moon in Pisces

The money trend continues, and will include funds, speculation, buying and selling of both commodities and shares. Investments will be built up. So also will the home or office – whatever is your stamping ground. Perhaps even both. As if this were not enough, a strong increase in your libido, so that passionate and sexual encounters are bound to happen now!

24 March: First Quarter in Cancer

After all that you were up to last week, you could rightly have wondered if I'd left anything out. It seems that I had, and that's made up for, this week. It's communication with a capital C – from all man's inventions like faxes, the Net, email and voice mail in constant use to even secret, closed-door deals and hush-hush consultations.

31 March: Full Moon in Libra

The first C of communication takes on two more – contacts and connections. It all started mid-March but the spectacular results have continued not only till now but may do so well into early July. Moon formed a trine with both Venus and Mercury, so double benefits. Does this explain it to your satisfaction?

8 April: Last quarter in Capricorn

All that you've striven for, hoped for, now seems to be handed to you on a platter. That's just one more P – the rest, are prestige, power, pelf, perks and promotions. All there, and the efforts you've put in seem well worth it now, don't they? Any legitimate tiredness or strain you may have felt is a thing of the past now.

16 April: New Moon in Aries

Journeys and study. That's the sum of it all this week. From travel to business, to spiritual journeys, to flights of the imagination. Also, research, original theories, deeper study, higher learning, whether for you or for your children. Religion and business partnerships trigger off the acquiring of knowledge.

22 April: First Quarter in Leo

It will be an uncanny similarity to the Moon quarter. You will take on the role of career, provider, nurturer, for the world at large, not just your family and dependents. It goes without saying that expenses will soar – they're bound to. Charity, philanthropy and welfare work will be your focus, though there should be a fair amount of travel.

30 April: Full Moon in Scorpio

There is a conjunction of Moon and Jupiter, the great benefactor of the planets, on the fourth house. This goes a long way towards offsetting the Sun–Saturn conjunction of the tenth house which could have proved harmful. All it does now is slow you down, make you introspect or even worry, suffer anxiety and tension.

8 May: Last Quarter in Aquarius

In your own sign, Moon's quarter lends a sharp, defining edge to everything you say and do. Reaching out to people and places could almost become an art form with you. Partnerships, including marriage are highlighted – your own or someone close to you. That's it, this quarter – it's the human angle!

15 May: New Moon in Taurus

Your work is all-important to you right now. It may be more than rewarding in itself, but now you will see the rewards that you deserve, and work for, come your way. By this, take it to mean success in the eyes of others and a matching rise in your own self-esteem.

22 May: First Quarter in Virgo

You will show a tremendous capacity for sheer grinding hard work this quarter too. It's like you've got a second windfall last week that will sustain you for some time. Better health too adds to this and much more charisma, reactivity, attractiveness to friends and the opposite sex.

29 May: Full Moon in Sagittarius

Children and creativity in every possible way as you declare 'time out'. Sports, holidays or vacations, recreation, hobbies, walks and shopping – all the things that add zest and gaiety to your life. All the good things of life, even higher study, research, music are in focus.

6 June: Last Quarter in Pisces

You now *have to* turn your attention to financial matters once again. In addition to your own personal shopping, there will be buying and selling, joint finance, loans, funds, capital raising – the whole gamut of financial activities in one form or another. At the same time your own career objectives will have to be defined, and domestic responsibilities and socializing dealt with.

13 June: New Moon in Gemini

You'll have to do two things in order to get the best deal for yourself this week. One is to improve your 'people skills', since meetings, collaborations and conferences will be vital, not just important. The other thing you need to do now is square up to your own responsibilities. This is not to say that you have been irresponsible.

20 June: First Quarter in Virgo

There will be lots to keep you busy right now. However, the main gains will come from your own inner changes. Once more, you go up the evolutionary ladder, with higher aims than before and your own ego and pride held well in check. You will focus on both, family and finances. These two Fs may well come together in a single form.

28 June: Full Moon in Capricorn

Property and family matters will be highlighted right through the coming month as well as in this quarter. It's your own work, as well as how you relate to people that will make things happen. Changes are likely in the family scene, and/or the set-up at home. You could even move house or have a change of locale.

6 July: Last Quarter in Aries

There will be plenty of social activities, family gatherings, happiness and relationships, especially after the powerful trine of Sun and Moon on 11 July. You may even have a wish-fulfilment or a dream being realized. Certainly, a long-held ambition will be met, and happily so, without hurt or offence to anyone.

13 July: New Moon in Cancer

All this month's trends are concretized and put into sharp focus this week. You will be earning from more than one source, but expenses will continue to cause you some anxiety. Notwithstanding, there is success in all that you hope to achieve. And that's saying a lot, isn't it? Ganesha nods.

19 July: First Quarter in Libra

Money worries will seem a thing of the past from this week. Travel, and a certain amount of ceremony, panache, will be part of your life right now. Ganesha warns you not to act like the Last of the Big Spenders. You are terribly prone to extravagance and when the money is easy, you splurge, throwing caution to the winds. And that's a no-no!

27 July: Full Moon in Aquarius

More travel this week too. Your birth month of August is the time for new beginnings, collaborations, tie-ups, partnerships. If a new one isn't started up, an existing tie-up will be injected with a fresh lease of life. The tremendously exciting extra will be the presence of love in your life, in all the overall scheme of things which imbues everything with a magic, and a touch of class.

4 August: Last Quarter in Taurus

Personal hang-ups, worries and hidden or overt complexes will all make their presence felt and you'll have to make an effort to conquer them. They are mighty power games in store for you this week – wheeling and dealing, getting things done, new ventures started, new projects not just passed, but funded. Family life too will be demanding – not necessarily in a bad way.

11 August: New Moon in Leo

Your innate charisma and confidence will resurface and be revived. Sheer daring and your own brave heart will help you get rid of the obstacles in your path. Your enemies and rivals may become active around this time, but you're ready to take them on. Acts of courage and daring are the essence of Leonine living. It's only necessary to caution you not to be foolhardy.

18 August: First Quarter in Scorpio

Family matters, house and home, and matters relating to both personal and inherited property keep you on your toes. You will be improving, adding on, redecorating, if necessary. This will all be part of how you wish to project your personal image, and there too you are in a search of a new look.

26 August: Full Moon in Pisces

Raising cash, acquiring wealth, organizing loans and funds for business, and also falling in love, having a passionate, if not steamy affair are all likely. So also, perhaps, a shift or move of the home/office premises, or perhaps setting up a love nest, home away from home. A legacy, lottery or sudden gain is likely.

3 September: Last Quarter in Gemini

All the things that thrill and entertain you, give you pleasure, are highlighted. Partying, dancing under the stars, adventure and other sports, wining and dining in right royal style are what you're doing this week, and loving it too. This mood of gaiety and fun will be part of your activities in daily life, as you waltz through the week to your own music.

9 September: New Moon in Virgo

You've had your time in the sun, and now it's not even 'business as usual', but business with an almighty bang. Finances will be the focus this week and there can be a lot of cutting deals, transactions and negotiations being engineered and, perhaps, settlement of legal cases or matters.

16 September: First Quarter in Sagittarius

Communication, interchange and exchange of ideas, information, opinions, news. Into this will also come journeys – for the rest of the year 2018 in fact. That's not all – you're searching for passion in relationships as well as religion. A passionate love affair or the occult, tantra and mantra, may prove to be the answer for you.

25 September: Full Moon in Aries

You have your focus, total attention and your sights firmly fixed on the future: your income-generating abilities, plans for the autumn of your life, for maintaining your lifestyle and improving upon it. You will travel, attend conferences, interviews, seminars, meetings, and have tie-ups and collaborations.

2 October: Last Quarter in Cancer

Visits to places of healing, community centres, welfare activities, larger causes and issues are in your plans. Also, most definitely, either journeys or plans to travel. There can be a certain amount of secret, arcane activities, hidden agendas, hush-hush meetings. You will not let your left hand know what your right hand is doing, in an attempt to guard your prospects.

9 October: New Moon in Libra

Both work and pleasure, almost in equal measure. You will take up a new line, a new subject or field of work, for both pleasure and profit. A lot of social interaction is foretold – foreign visitors, house guests, friends dropping by. Intellectual brilliance, a desire to achieve, to challenge and outrun your own self will have you going places.

16 October: First Quarter in Capricorn

There's a gigantic leap in work, creativity, profession. There will be a lot of involvement with home and family – in terms of older people – as well. The home may have an addition; an overall improvement or renovation. Borrowing, funds, buying, selling too.

24 October: Full Moon in Taurus

A single word sums up this week and the month to come, and that word is satisfaction – sweet and simple! In your work, vocation, specialization, there will be both advancement and job satisfaction. Finances too, and in addition, you see that your blueprints for the future are taking concrete shape.

31 October: Last Quarter in Leo

You will be alert, ready, poised for the kill, the lord of the jungle of modern civilization, living up to your namesake, the lion. Your positive outlook will be tailor-made for action, productive work, good family bonding. Underlying this will be much better health and reserves of energy that help you get things done.

7 November: New Moon in Scorpio

You can see now that there is a direction of your choosing where all your activities are heading, and it's a very satisfying feeling, indeed. It makes for more leisure time, greater closeness in family ties. Your family both plays and prays together, right now. Your home will get a facelift or makeover, and there will be a fair amount of buying and selling – either things for the home, or stocks or shares or even both.

15 November: First Quarter in Aquarius

In your own birth sign, it's a time when you call the shots, make the ground rules, and play to win. Romance brings a welcome whiff of gaiety and joy. There is bonding at all levels – purely personal, romantic, amorous, family – you name it. Engagements and/or weddings may originate from this week. Ganesha plays Cupid.

23 November: Full Moon in Gemini

There will be entertainment, group activity, romance, creativity at white heat, pleasure, bonding with loved ones. You will feel loved and cared for. A wish-fulfilment or dream come true too, says Ganesha, for good measure. Where's the catch? You might as well ask. Be fair and impartial, if you can't stay out of it!

30 November: Last Quarter in Virgo

It's time to work hard, since the results you've striven for are so much within your reach. The year 2018 has been good for you, especially the last quarter of it. Now too there can be sudden gains, windfalls, lotteries. Also, a welcome addition to the family, even perhaps a new birth. Don't give in to the temptation to be complacent or too self-willed.

7 December: New Moon in Sagittarius

You will get, and truly deserve, the respect of others. Your creativity and talents will scale dazzling new heights. Work and play find you excelling at both. Your popularity, credit, social position and standing touch new heights too. You have your own ingenuity, positive and sharing attitude to thank for, making all this come to pass.

15 December: First Quarter in Pisces

You will keep your cool, no matter what. You will be loved, or at least liked, warts and all. Plenty of activity, in terms of raising finances, loans, funds, deals to be negotiated and perhaps a shift or office move. Don't harbour wrong emotions and yet be a stickler for your rights, your freedom, your leisure, if you feel they are threatened.

22 December: Full Moon in Cancer

Let me just say – get set to make very positive but realistic plans for the millennium, or at least the year to come. You will have plenty of activity, lots of action and yet time to think, and think deeply indeed, amidst the storm of things that you undertake. The luck of the draw will favour you in tricky situations.

29 December: Last Quarter in Libra

It is a time for brilliance, scintillating social interaction, sparkling at parties and/or on the cocktail circuit. Imagination, inventiveness, entertainment are all at white heat – therefore some marvellous creativity. An incredible originality in your approach even to the most humdrum activities from cookery to games, to love-making, to sports, to amusements.

VIRGO

23 August–22 September

Virgo is reserved, modest, practical, discriminating and industrious, analytical and painstaking, seeking to know and understand. Your creative juices will flood the whole world. The word 'joy' best sums up the celebration of life; of daring and caring despite the odds. Ganesha says home, house, work, status, prestige, parents, in-laws, travel will keep you on your 'twinkling toes' in 2018.

- **Element:** Earth
- **Ruling planet:** Mercury
- **Colours:** Earth tones, ochre, orange, yellow
- **Gems:** Agate, hyacinth (jacinth)
- **Metal:** Quicksilver
- **Scents:** Lavender, lilac, lily of the valley
- **Quality:** Mutability (=flexibility)
- **Quality most needed for balance:** A broader perspective
- **Strongest virtues:** Mental agility, analytical skills, ability to pay attention to detail, healing powers

- **Deepest needs:** To be useful and productive
- **Characteristics to avoid:** Destructive criticism
- **Day:** Wednesday
- **Number:** Five
- **Flowers:** Buttercup, pansy, forget-me-not, morning glory, aster, mimosa
- **Trees:** Hazel, horse chestnut, and all nut-bearing trees
- **Foods:** Potatoes, carrots, turnips, all vegetables grown under the earth; also nuts of all varieties

Special Message from Bejan and Nastur: In ancient times Virgo, Libra and Scorpio were one sign. My special observation is that all these three signs are very choosy and fussy about food and health and may have phobias. I repeat that they *may* have phobias. I do not say that all of them have definite phobias. A Virgo woman is usually aware of health and hygiene issues, especially when it concerns cutting-edge research.

JUPITER

Jupiter will be in your third angle from 10 October 2017 to 8 November 2018. Jupiter stands for good luck, success and expansion. The additional goodies of Jupiter will be courage and valour, physical fitness, hobbies, talent, education, good qualities, longevity of parents, tolerance, capability, quality and nature of food, selfishness, sports, fights, refuge, trading, dreams, sorrows, stability of mind, the neighbourhood, near relations, friends, army, inheritance, ornaments, cleverness, short journeys. Wow! What a list!

The additional highlights are:

a) This is the right time to take crash course in matters which interest you, develop self-expression, and cultivate opinions.

b) Play chess or bridge, enter quiz shows, Sudoku contests, in short, all mental games.

c) Learn to get along with relatives and neighbours.

d) Try not to have mental strain, because this is where you are weak and therefore vulnerable; be ready to listen to others, though I know you are both able and discriminating.

e) Enrich your mind and enhance your knowledge.

I have mentioned this in earlier writings. Major climatic changes are happening, with dire consequences on our planet. Jupiter in third angle shows research, intelligence and thrust to help people realize that we are the family of man. Ganesha says, Jupiter in your third angle could help enhance memory and the processing of talk. More accurate weather/climate and geological predictions could perhaps be made too. Perhaps even artificial intelligence could be the final gift of Jupiter in the third angle. All these could be the brainchild or handiwork of your sign.

SATURN

Rationality and romance are born enemies. Why? Love is blind. The heart has its reasons which the mind never understands. But perhaps in your case there may be unique blending of romance and finance. I am writing it in the days of demonetization, namely, 9 December 2016.

By Western astrology, Saturn will be in your fifth angle from 21 December 2017 to 22 March 2020. The actual results of it will be:

1.   Tremendous creativity;
2.   A very wide choice in life.

Let us first take tremendous creativity. In this, the following features will be included: a) pleasurable pursuits and hobbies; b) children and other loved ones; c) executive ability; d) romance; e) strengthening bonds of affection; f) highlighting social activities; g) seeing things in a new light, having faith in the future.

Ganesha says, Saturn in the fifth angle also gives pain, separation and shocks in the above matters. The home could be disturbed and disrupted. In short, Saturn will give you mixed results. Be ready to laugh and cry in the same breath.

You Virgos (and Geminis too) are experts in contacts and communication, each in his/her own way. Mercury is your boss planet. Mercury helps you in every possible way. From 1 to 17 January, 11 February to 6 March: journeys and religion; 31 March to 24 April: long-distance connections and ceremonies; 20 May to 13 June: combining home and work; 10 July to 6 August: confidence, courage, journeys, research; 9 September to 31 October: all-round personality like Virat Kohli. And once again, from 3 to 31 December: house, home, property. Let me make it very clear to you that this is only a general reading and therefore it will not apply completely and very accurately to you. If it does, consider it as Ganesha's grace.

URANUS

Uranus will move in and out of your health sector giving you mixed results. But if you have a chronic health problem it should go away by the end of 2019 latest. Reiki, dowsing, yoga, positive thinking, the use of colours, water therapy, mud bath, sauna bath – yes all these will help you in terms of wholeness and well-being.

NEPTUNE

Neptune will make your heart hum like a guitar and you might sing like a bird of paradise. After a time, there could be a few thorns in your throat also. Why? Neptune is both reality and illusion. But overall, Neptune will help you in terms of unusual partnerships, friends, romance, journeys. You are advised to stay away from drinks and drugs for your own good.

PLUTO

Pluto is the punch of the late Muhammad Ali, the world's greatest boxer. Pluto makes you glamorous, sexy, appealing and charming. Use it wisely and well

MONTHLY ROUND-UPS

January: You will be off and away to a really flying start, says Ganesha, and as you know, well begun is half done; **February** and **March:** Expenses but also progress, therefore, mixed results; **April:** Excellent for finances and family affairs and earned income; **May:** Reaching out to people and places by all media of transport and communication; **June:** Important for peace, buying/selling/renovating/decorating, a home away from home; **July**: Love, romance, the luck of the draw, creativity and children, family and fun and fortune; **August**: Health, employment, pets, servants and colleagues and a few problems connected with these; **September**: Love and hate, marriage and making merry, but paradoxically, in a few cases, separation and legal cases, and that is why life is so complex, uncertain, full of contradictions and surprises; **October**: Funds, loans, capital formation, money matters, shopping; **November**: Inspiration, journeys, name and fame, good luck; **December**: Power, prestige, parents, profession, awards and rewards, money, home, house and office.

HAPPINESS QUOTA: 87 per cent

WEEKLY REVIEW (BY PHASES OF THE MOON)

2 January: Full Moon in Cancer

You're upwardly mobile, most definitely so in terms of money, entertaining, social life. Gains in power, prestige, status too. Also, time for family outings, bonding with spouse and children and friends. There can be a tendency to overindulge in all pleasures of the flesh.

8 January: Last Quarter in Libra

Careful handling of finances and some clever moves will maintain the upward trend of last week, in money matters and other spheres as well. You have a fine start to the year, Virgos, and it may prevail right through the year, barring a few hiccups, of course. It happens in all families and you'll take it in your stride.

17 January: New Moon in Capricorn

You may be justified in thinking you've never had it so good. All the Ps – power, prestige, promotion, pelf, perks, position – are yours for the taking. And take them you will, believe me. As if these were not enough, there may even be romance, falling genuinely in love, if you're still young at heart and fancy-free.

24 January: First Quarter in Taurus

You've got more than your share to keep you busy and happy, but now there will be the added benefit of spirituality, religion, tantra and mantra. Your mind soars to new heights. Money matters will be good – collaborations, deals, mergers will click. A change of residence or job could be on the cards as part of the deal.

31 January: Full Moon in Leo

Secret matters, hushed negotiations, deals and behind-the-scene activities will definitely be there in some form or other. You will also be more withdrawn from the world, seeking out lonely places or at least, showing a desire for solitude. Contrarily enough, at the same time, a fair amount of travelling, business and professional interaction, meeting the right people and sparkling social interaction.

7 February: Last Quarter in Scorpio

Finances will suddenly be easy, so will the flow of cash for both domestic and office/business needs. There will be growth and expansion of work. Physically, health is somewhat better and there will be warmth in relationships, family ties, marital harmony too. All this because of your own inner growth and mentality, the readiness to reach out.

15 February: New Moon in Aquarius

Work is in the spotlight, and you perform with your usual Virgo precision and efficiency. Novel ideas, avant-garde projects, even fresh collaborations will take off, and pending ones successfully completed. Ways and means of getting an extra income, making that extra buck, will come to you, in a flash of inspiration.

23 February: First Quarter in Gemini

You've got your eye on the main chance, all right, in your career or profession. A change of job, town or city, transfer or deputation to another department could well materialize. The change of scene could even be a promotion but there should be much advancement and progress in your career graph right now.

2 March: Full Moon in Virgo

Your public image and private persona shine forth like a newly minted coin. It's your profession/job/career/business that you'll shine the most in, though some of the glitter rubs off on to family life as well. You will be a true representative of the success and dynamism that most people aspire for these days.

9 March: Last Quarter in Sagittarius

It's your family, your roots, that are important for you, and your home is the centre of the universe, in that sense. Parents, in-laws and older relatives will have your care and attention lavished on them, as also the house and home, despite a certain amount of time spent away from it in travel.

17 March: New Moon in Pisces

You go all out to realize your ambition and make future plans a reality, both professionally and domestically. And you're on the brink of achieving it all, this week, if not already there in some ways. Of course, the temptation to overdo things, take on more than you can cope with is to be avoided, and rest and relaxation will be more necessary than ever.

24 March: First Quarter in Cancer

It's warm companionship, togetherness and love that warm the cockles of your heart this week and you're not just in the mood to relax but to party and socialize as well. Virgos can often be party animals. At any rate, they need hectic social life, interaction with friends and even acquaintances to feel they're really alive. And you're no exception.

31 March: Full Moon in Libra

The two Fs of family and finance are still the main focus. Some family matters will need to be disentangled on an urgent basis right now, though they've been on the back burner while you were caught up with work and career demands. These issues could well pertain to family, money or property. You will be in a daring mood in business transactions and money matters.

8 April: Last Quarter in Capricorn

You see-saw between the world of material things and that of relationships, so this time it's ties, bonds, relationships once again. It's a happy time in terms of outings, entertainment, luck investments, creativity in hobbies and specially in your joy from your children. The extra bonus will be the total commitment and joy from that special someone in your life/ heart – your true love.

16 April: New Moon in Aries

You'll be almost hyperactive in both work and recreation in equal measure. It's a time for risk taking for both love and money. Two time-tested sayings – 'Fortune favours the brave' and 'Faint heart never won fair lady' just about sum up this quarter for Virgos. Also, a bit of socializing, a dash of travel, and hectic activity all round!

22 April: First Quarter in Leo

On the work front, your public relations and people skills will be mind-boggling. You will achieve targets easily, meet deadlines, accomplish difficult missions and assignments with deceptive ease. You'll get on 'swimmingly' with people, as Bertie Wooster would have said, and that is the secret of your success.

30 April: Full Moon in Scorpio

There'll be expenses that go off into the outer hemisphere, they're so high, but income will match, so there could, really speaking, be no money worries. Part of the expenses could well be gadgets, comforts and luxuries for the home, that is equally in focus this quarter. A phase that you should be thankful for has prevailed for you for the last few weeks.

8 May: Last Quarter in Aquarius

There's no stopping you while you're on a roll, as Saurav Ganguly was when he broke the record at the World Cup League match at Taunton, England. Distinguished gatherings, PR exercises, friends in high places, and in the highest (political?) circles will ensure that nothing can stop your meteoric rise.

15 May: New Moon in Taurus

Journeys will yield pleasure and profit, so too will romance, marriage, or getting married – more pleasure, I'm not so sure about profit! Your public image will shine forth. Conferences, meets, seminars, collaborations will have you participating brilliantly, and having a whale of a time doing it. More power to you, says Ganesha's devotee.

22 May: First Quarter in Virgo

Secret deals, closed-door meetings, arcane and esoteric activities and pursuits will be most important in this period. A secret love affair or liaison, perhaps, also. With this kind of cloak-and-dagger stuff, and hidden romance, your expenses will be very high indeed. It's expensive to have mistresses or play cops and robbers, isn't it?

29 May: Full Moon in Sagittarius

You will throw out all the excitement and high living from your lifestyle and concentrate on home and family, a quiet life, the joys of domesticity and slippers warming on the hearth. You're still a daring risk taker in matters financial, though, and investments and speculation will be very, very lucrative.

6 June: Last Quarter in Pisces

To make all your ambitions and dreams a reality, you'll have to work your butt off! And you're able and willing, this period. Travel with a stopover, maybe, and ties and collaborations. There will be heightened activity in this period since it's in your birth sign. What will also be majorly important will be partnerships, whether old or new, professional or personal.

13 June: New Moon in Gemini

You'll be impressive at work, in your office/factory/business premises. It's at your workplace that you're at your best this week, though even at play and pleasure pursuits, you come a close second. There is a certain intensity in all that you undertake. Whatever, you make all the right moves, say and do all the right things, with Ganesha's inspiration.

20 June: First Quarter in Virgo

It's a phase when you want to review your life, reassess your values, priorities and focus, even while you continue to work without letting up on your standards. It's your home and family that get your attention, and there may be an intensely personal matter to resolve as well. A long-cherished dream may come true now.

28 June: Full Moon in Capricorn

In this period the glitter and sparkle are even more wonderful. Here's how it goes: a) achievements – advertising, the arts, information technology, research, academics all do brilliantly; b) happiness in personal life – laughter, good friends, romance, love and marriage; c) success – good partnerships, deals made now are crowned with great profit and gain.

6 July: Last Quarter in Aries

Home and family may need some reorganizing. You will need a lot of funds for domestic affairs, so joint finance, marital funds and accounts will have to be dealt with, along with career demands. There may be a financial settlement to be made and domestic responsibilities to be fulfilled. You need not shelve your own individual career aspirations to do so.

13 July: New Moon in Cancer

It's a time for not money, or monetary gain, but truly hitting the jackpot in life, in terms of both advancement and wealth, serious money. You will have it all – power, position, prestige and pelf. Ganesha's bounty will have no limits for you, at least in material terms.

19 July: First Quarter in Libra

You'll have to pack more activity into this phase of your life than ever before, and the main thrust, focus, goal and result, will be money. The colour of money influences all your activities, at home, in the office, even with pets and children and certainly love and romance and marriage, not to mention your social life.

27 July: Full Moon in Aquarius

A trend of sheer, mind-blowing hard work is coupled with equally mind-blowing success in love, romance, moneymaking. In addition, you'll be drawn to religion, tantra and mantra, prayer and meditation for rest, relaxation and inspiration. Even success can be tiring, as I'm sure you'll be discovering by now. This will be the trend for the next few weeks.

4 August: Last Quarter in Taurus

It's socializing with a bang, panache and style. You will truly have a ball this week. Business and public relations, ceremonies and functions, parties, games and sports, ties and collaborations. You also make money in the bargain! But rest, health care and an improved routine, and diet will prove to be more necessary than ever.

11 August: New Moon in Leo

Dealing with sickness, visits to the hospitals – for yourself or someone close to you – will make you stop in your tracks and think. So also will the mind-boggling expenses. It could be that you have not heeded my warning of last week. In any case, you will want to reassess the way your life is going, wonderful as it may be, and try for a different focus or goal and a more laid-back approach.

18 August: First Quarter in Scorpio

There will be a remarkable coming together of family members in your scheme of things. Your brothers, sisters, close relatives will mean much to you. There will be a fair amount of travel and expansion of the mind – learning a new skill, computer technology, higher study, research, further qualifications. This will all prove to be a more or less direct result of the last week's soul-searching.

26 August: Full Moon in Pisces

A period of intense activity. This is usual in the birth month of all signs. There will be skills and achievements galore, some dreams coming true, ambitions realized but this kind of dazzling success that you have enjoyed since May excites envy, jealousy, even enmity in others. You will need to watch out, particularly in money matters where you must *not*, repeat *not*, go anywhere near doubtful, fraudulent deals.

3 September: Last Quarter in Gemini

It is only now that the necessity of being prepared for any eventuality makes you appreciate the worth of true values, good motives and righteous living. It's not that you haven't done so earlier, but now it becomes a part of your life in a way never before experienced, even by you, perfection-loving Virgo. Your commitment to hard work continues and is built in to this approach to life.

9 September: New Moon in Virgo

Caring, sharing, attachments, peace, excellence, harmony – all come together for you. Your family, loved ones, and particularly your spouse, will be 'the be-all and end-all' of your life. I can't express it better than in this famous phrase of William Shakespeare's. This conviction will guide all your actions and activities, even love and romance in the future.

16 September: First Quarter in Sagittarius

You will be truly original, inventive and ingenious in your approach to life and living, even New Age living. The home and hearth, your own property or piece of earth, will come in for renovation, restoration, care. You will be marvellous too at all kinds of communication, but most of all in family issues where you display wisdom tempered with affection.

25 September: Full Moon in Aries

A tremendous burst of power, greatness and glory. It will be centred around religion, money, sex and passion – perhaps all of them! This is a time when you are a winner in the game of life, but have to pay for the chips you gamble with. Health worries, the slight changes because of an accident may need to be watched out for, warns Ganesha.

2 October: Last Quarter in Cancer

You will experience a letting up of the tensions and worries that come to you. You will relax, rejuvenate yourself. (This can be done at any age.) Good company, friends, socializing, merrymaking and laughter, outings and sports – all these activities contribute in no small measure. Added to this will be success in business/profession.

9 October: New Moon in Libra

The three Fs – food, family and of course, finance. But here they need a little explaining. Let's start with: a) Food – implying entertaining and being entertained, dining out, the hospitality industry, even diet care, hotels, restaurants, nutrition consultation; b) Family – matters not involving just your immediate family and siblings, but also extended family, in-laws, your ancestors, your roots and your attachment to them.

16 October: First Quarter in Capricorn

It will be just people for you this period. Personal relationships are everything to you, right now. These will necessarily show complete involvement in your individual worth and creativity, your children's affairs, activities, pursuits and finally domestic and family issues. All of these will be important to you, and your role in them will be equally important and vital. That's it.

24 October: Full Moon in Taurus

The trend which set in with the last new moon phase extends over and into this month as well. Wish-fulfilment, dreams coming true; a total self-improvement campaign from clothes and hairstyle to home. Also important will be journeys and ceremonies – religious and otherwise, and of course, the best for the last – fireworks in terms of intuition, perception, strokes of pure genius.

31 October: Last Quarter in Leo

Journeys and relationships are most important for you. With travel comes a certain distancing yourself from this world you live in, a touch of world-weariness, ennui, disillusionment. It's only the reaching out to places and people that will help you overcome this, as well as the sense of aloneness that could overwhelm you. Ganesha will give you solace – he always does.

7 November: New Moon in Scorpio

You have put the past quarter's phase behind you, performing brilliantly at interviews, examinations, tests of skill and/or mental agility and ability. There's much happiness from your children too to pull you out of the doldrums and finally, lots of travel as well. You do it all with typical Virgo thoroughness and excellence.

15 November: First Quarter in Aquarius

Money matters and those concerning dependents will be where you try out your impressive skills at management, the attempt to put the entire world in order. Money matters will relate to loans and funds for projects, arranging for capital, investments for social work in particular. Social ills and anomalies will be attacked head-on by you now.

23 November: Full Moon in Gemini

Perks, promotions, prospects, position and power are the five Ps from now till the end of 2018. That's the millennium's gift to you, all given a kick-start but showing results now. Respect, recognition, rewards, they're all there. Learn to be grateful, says Ganesha and don't criticize others not so lucky as you are. Nothing succeeds like success, they say, but kindness to less successful people succeeds even more.

30 November: Last Quarter in Virgo

There will be a lot of idealism in your attitudes now, particularly regarding the values of self-help and hard work and sheer striving for excellence. All of which are a necessary part of your personality and mental make-up. You'll incorporate all of this in your life in 'the daily round, the common task' and lift beyond the ordinary.

7 December: New Moon in Sagittarius

A new line of work, alongside your own, that you had undertaken earlier in the year, could prove to be more absorbing and interesting. So also your public image, how others see you, how you project yourself to the whole wide world. Your inner self will remain largely hidden, especially the lofty ideals and sentiments that you have acquired. It's only to a chosen few that you show your true self, or let down your guard.

15 December: First Quarter in Pisces

You'll hold out the olive branch to your enemies, get in touch with long-lost relatives, long-forgotten friends and visit childhood haunts in a trip down memory lane. People will be important, if not everything now as you build bridges of entente cordiale. So also will love and romance – cosy twosomes against the chill of winter! Official and private functions and ceremonies will keep you busy, and happy too.

22 December: Full Moon in Cancer

You will have all the three cardinal virtues of faith, hope and charity in your heart as you look at 2,000 years of the Christian era. Also, a look ahead at the dawn of the next 1,000 years of enlightenment, hope for the future and a better world order. It's not idle thoughts and hopes though. You're ready to roll up your sleeves and get ready to work to make it all happen. More power to you, my brother in mankind, say Ganesha and I.

29 December: Last Quarter in Libra

The euphoria generated by your achievements, activities, honour and reputation, now brings tremendous gains in terms of both warm friendship and material advancement, so that you feel fulfilled, satisfied, pleased with life. It is however, a time to steer clear of involvement in money matters with friends, associates or colleagues. All in all, you will be more friendly, more magnanimous, but also more extravagant.

LIBRA

23 September–22 October

Life can be a necklace of glittering rubies and diamonds, each gem in its own brilliance, and dancing in radiance with all the others.

- **Element:** Air
- **Ruling planet:** Venus
- **Colours:** Blue, jade green
- **Metal:** Copper
- **Scents:** Almond, rose, vanilla, violet
- **Quality:** Cardinal (=activity)
- **Deepest needs:** Love, romance, social harmony
- **Characteristics to avoid:** Violating what is right in order to be socially accepted
- **Day:** Friday

Special Message from Bejan and Nastur: In ancient times Virgo, Libra and Scorpio were one sign. My special observation is that all these three signs are very choosy and fussy about food, health and may have phobias. I repeat that they *may* have phobias. I do not say that all of them have definite phobias. Librans have an inherent need to act democratically, diplomatically and fairly. Adversely afflicted, they have trouble in making decisions and may lose themselves in sensual pleasures. In highly evolved Librans, the human mind finds the perfect blend between balance and discretions.

JUPITER

Jupiter will be in your second angle from 10 October 2017 to 8 November 2018. Jupiter is the heavyweight of the zodiac. Jupiter has everything to do with finance, family, food, taste, clothes, knowledge, education, servants, wealth, physical enjoyments, buying and selling, earning through your own efforts and acquisitions from father. Jupiter actually gives you a silver tongue as the Americans say. So, dear suave and diplomatic Librans, you know what to expect from Jupiter in 2018. Wow!

SATURN

By Western astrology, Saturn will be in your fourth angle from 21 December 2017 to 22 March 2020. Saturn is a spoilsport, a killjoy, a wet blanket. In other words, Saturn spoils the fun and the joy of life. Therefore, you will not get all the happy results of the fourth house. For elderly people, Saturn in the fourth angle will mark the end of a relationship which has been going on for a long time. The emphasis will very definitely be on local, family and domestic frontiers. Saturn is a lame old man. Therefore, Saturn represents old people like parents and elders. Saturn is also a teacher. Therefore, Saturn also represents gurus and mentors. Saturn, by both Indian and Western astrology, stands for duties and responsibilities. So, it is very clear that your responsibilities and duties will increase many times over. Be prepared to shoulder them. You Librans have balance and poise. It will help you in every possible way.

If you are young at heart you can start making a blueprint of your profession and accomplishments. It will be the right time to amend and stitch up all pending issues and matters. Also, if you have made commitments, it is time to fulfil them.

Saturn by nature is objective and rational and does not like to be too personal and subjective. I would naturally advice you not be very personal and as far as possible be objective, rational, clear-headed. The other features are house, home, property, renovation and decoration, alteration, mining, gardening, farming. The list is endless. I will make it very simple. Anything to do with land and property will come into sharp focus. I am sure you do understand this very well.

For you Librans, Venus, the planet of beauty, money, honey, is the main planet. Venus will help you in creativity hobbies from 18 January to 12 February and from 7 to 30 March. Relationships will matter the most. From 25 April to 19 May journeys, travel, ceremonies, foreign affairs, matters related to parents will claim your attention. From 14 June to 9 July you will combine business and pleasure, entertainment and profit. This is a really a fine period for you. From 7 August to 8 September you will try to analyse and introspect your own self, and at the same time fan out to other people. In other words, you will be doing many things at the same time. The best part of it is that this last prediction will be repeated between 1 November to 2 December for you.

In 2018, Saturn and Jupiter will be in an excellent formation. Therefore, I suggest that you should try to get the best out of the year. You should ring it dry.

URANUS

On and after 4 March 2019 Uranus moves out of your seventh angle. This is a blessing. The reason is Uranus screws up your relationships in one way or another. Uranus disrupts and changes everything. In other words, the year 2018 will be the last one of changes. These changes could mean separations, lawsuits, legal affairs, opposition to parents and so on. Fortunately, you Librans are charming and polished, and therefore you will be hurt less than those of other signs by Uranus.

NEPTUNE

Neptune will be in your eighth angle till 2024. But in 2018, very specially, Neptune will turn on your intuition, imagination, psychic powers, dreams and so on. Also, Neptune will augment your income by different sources and that is certainly very important. These sources could be rent, factory, industry, job, profession, business, freelancing. To put it simply you will get money in different ways.

PLUTO

Pluto walks beside Saturn in your fourth angle and Pluto helps Saturn to walk a little faster and give quicker results. Please read Saturn in your fourth angle once again. Everything said there will work at a quicker pace and be more beneficial at least by 50 per cent or so. Your former professor of English, now eighty-six years old, cannot resist the temptation of giving marks.

MONTHLY ROUND-UPS

January: House, home, family; **February:** Romance, children, creativity; **March:** Work and health improvement measures; **April:** Marriage, relationships, contacts, trips, ties and opposition; **May:** Loans, funds, health, taxes, accidents, legal matters; **June:** Publicity, publishing, fame, religious rites, matters to do with parents and in-laws; **July:** Parents, in-laws, work, rewards, family, the effort you do put in; **August:** Contacts and group activities, gains and joy; **September:** Expenses, health, but also God's grace and success in ventures and fine connections, collaborations; **October:** Confidence, success, charm; **November:** Finances, family, food, fortune, the four Fs, **December:** Communication and contacts at all levels.

HAPPINESS QUOTA: 76 per cent

WEEKLY REVIEW (BY PHASES OF THE MOON)

2 January: Full Moon in Cancer

You will be striving to achieve right from the word 'go'. You want to have the position and clout to go your own way, do what you like best. All this needs the power (either in terms of social/family status or money) and that's what you set out to get. For this, hard work is the only answer and that's what you're doing, in the new millennium, but with a set purpose in mind.

8 January: Last Quarter in Libra

The word I spoke of, just above, centres on creative pursuits – always a focal point for Librans, in some form or other – as a means of earning. Hobbies too will be equally important. Your main concern will be your family, particularly your children, though parents and in-laws too play an important role. Moneymaking, in terms of speculation, playing the stock market, will be favoured, but don't be foolhardy.

17 January: New Moon in Capricorn

Once again family matters, the health of older relatives, parents and in-laws is focused. Also, equally important will be matters pertaining to your house and property as a family holding. Hassles or problems not of your making but still yours to sort out will take time, effort, hard work, and needless to say, money as well. You've got your hands full this quarter. Your own health too will need safeguarding.

24 January: First Quarter in Taurus

There's a tremendous lightening up of the environment you're living in, a breath of spring in the heart of winter. I'm talking now about love and romance, joy, gaiety, laughter. You interact with people now, no longer ploughing a lonely furrow. Good times, the social whirligig, bring a measure of happiness, and ease the burdens you were weighed down by.

31 January: Full Moon in Leo

You will now shift your orientation from the social and family scene. It's money that will concern and occupy you, in terms of funds and investments, lending and borrowing for your own projects and enterprises. Your interactions with people will have to be at their best. Don't vitiate the atmosphere with confrontations, showdowns that can be avoided with tact. It's not the time to feel threatened by others. You need people for your own advancement, says Ganesha.

7 February: Last Quarter in Scorpio

Once again, money matters this week too. You'll have to attend to buying and selling, possessions and valuables, property and liquid assets. Don't be bulldozed into doing something you don't want to or let others trespass in your path. Family matters will demand that you be gentle but firm and stick up for yourself. Tact and charm will come in more handy for personal affairs that clamour for your attention. Ganesha warns you – a busy week.

15 February: New Moon in Aquarius

It's a time to love and be loved, to have that touch of romance and moonlight in your life. And that's something that Librans can really excel at. It's part of their charming, caressing ways – both sexes, not just Libran women. Fun, recreation and joy with children, pleasure and the leisure to chase it. Sounds like dream time? But there's the harsh reality of money matters to be dealt with, investments to be made.

23 February: First Quarter in Gemini

Trade and travel will keep you more than busy. Yet you find the time since you already have the inclination towards higher concerns like world laws, an order in the universe, justice for mankind. Spirituality, New Age concepts and values could easily be your forte now.

2 March: Full Moon in Virgo

It'll be a time of worries for you. Home affairs and ever-rising demands on your purse keep your nose to the grindstone. Your mind and heart, though, soar to new heights of God realization, realization of the oneness of God and Self, and searching within for both. A life of meditation, quietude, contemplation will be doubly attractive. This trend will prevail for some weeks to come.

9 March: Last Quarter in Sagittarius

Your contemplative tendencies will take a back seat for the moment. There will be worries in juxtaposition with wish-fulfilment and dreams realized. Love and hate come to you in equal measure too. In addition, there will be a fairly large amount of social interaction and also much activity at the workplace. All in all, to call it a busy week would be an understatement.

17 March: New Moon in Pisces

Your work, your own creative talents and productivity will figure largely now. Also, and this will be an 'ongoing exercise' in modern office jargon, larger issues and social causes. In the money angle, there is an easing of tension as loans and funds come through. But you need to exercise care and control over your food habits and health. Keep a watch over your temper and your tongue, though.

24 March: First Quarter in Cancer

All your hard work, I might even say your Herculean efforts of the past, will start paying off now, especially in the workplace. In relationships, there can be harsh words, frayed tempers to watch for, to prevent relationships from turning bitter. The health of an older relative or parents can cause you many anxious moments too. Money-wise, it's a time when you're reasonably flush with funds, so it eases the stress. Social standing, perks and benefits get a boost too.

31 March: Full Moon in Libra

It's a time when nothing can stop your personal progress. I'm saying this at the outset with a purpose. You can just decide not to be too domineering and assertive, creating animosity where none exists. It's not a good time in the sense that betrayals, back-stabbing, or let-downs could happen anyway. What you need now is emotional balance.

8 April: Last Quarter in Capricorn

You will have to deal, once again, with family matters, the house and home, property. Renovation, decoration, construction, extension may be necessary. You change from within and this is reflected in the change for the better in relations with family and relatives, and in domestic issues. Both could hitherto have been more than bothersome.

16 April: New Moon in Aries

Finance and romance, now. In matters financial it will be trade, buying and selling, and also partnerships, tie-ups, collaborations that are important. Legal issues, enforcement of the law, will also be important. Short journeys are likely. I'm sure I don't have to spell out the details vis-à-vis romance. You can do it yourself!

22 April: First quarter in Leo

There will, once again, be both happy times and hard work. Your Libran tendency will be to have both in equal measure but it can be a 60:40 ratio, with the balance tilting either way, depending on your personal horoscope. The bad news is that there could be concern about an older person in the family – health-wise.

30 April: Full Moon in Scorpio

A fresh new look comes into your life – the glitter of money. There are several different ways in which you could find yourself pursuing the making of money – buying and selling, also contracts, negotiations, even commission agencies. You could be signing legal documents, instruments of understanding, handling loans. Also, there will be the glamour of a new, fashionable wardrobe and a healthy amount of entertaining.

8 May: Last Quarter in Aquarius

There is a shift towards better times now. Better health, better prospects, also the mindset which lets you enjoy parties, social gatherings, interaction with children. Appreciate the arts, enjoy theatre, music, exhibitions, as well as your own individual interests and hobbies. The placing I spoke of at the outset may influence your attitude to others – resentment of others, or lack of consideration and care for loved ones.

15 May: New Moon in Taurus

Love and money, usually considered the two motivating factors the world over, are yours too. Money matters will revolve around loans, joint finance, shopping, investments. Basically, more opportunities to make money – perhaps a job switch. You surely don't need to have the details of the love angle spelt out, but even so the tilt is more towards passion, sex, rather than love.

22 May: First Quarter in Virgo

Your improved financial resources now permit you to indulge yourself, doing the things that please you. Hobbies, quality time and interaction with both children and friends, and above all, love. Perhaps an affair, a liaison or a lifetime bond. This will of course depend on the individual natal horoscope.

29 May: Full Moon in Sagittarius

Other things were going for you in a wonderful way last month. Now, it's relationships and communication; interaction with friends, neighbours, relatives or the whole wide world; the signing of contracts; or just correspondence and contacts; and of course, the entire range of media available in the world of information technology.

6 June: Last Quarter in Pisces

It's time for action for you now, Libran, and sheer grinding hard work. The sphere will be the electronic media, information technology, website of your own. The time is favourable for you to successfully launch a new venture/project/enterprise based on new technology. If nothing else, perhaps just streamlining and updating your work system, office procedures, what have you, for greater efficiency and better communication.

13 June: New Moon in Gemini

The action continues this week too. New fields of study, new avenues of research, inventions, innovations. The key word, you may have noticed, is *new*. Travel is a foregone conclusion. Also, a means of broadening your mind to new vistas of knowledge. You may have to attend interviews, conferences or a meeting, perhaps even chair a committee. The world at large beckons and draws you nearer.

20 June: First Quarter in Virgo

Your mood undergoes a sea change – a whole new perspective is what you have. Contemplation and isolation draw you more. Seas, water sources like rivers and lakes will attract you. You will feel both tired, world-weary and restless. This could have been building up over the past few weeks. On a practical level, there could be trade and connections overseas, foreign collaborations that may be fruitful.

28 June: Full Moon in Capricorn

Having thought things through in the quiet you were craving. You realize that for you home is where the heart is, in a slightly different twist to this saying. Family, bonding with loved ones, close relatives, the joys of home comforts, domestic bliss and ties are what you seek. Ties could also be with someone older and wiser.

6 July: Last Quarter in Aries

The give-and-take trend of the last quarter could be a monthly trend. Other ties like legal accords, collaborations and partnerships may now develop. These could cover both home and work. There is much satisfaction for you, even a degree of pleasure in both work and family matters. Ganesha has blessed you in an unobtrusive, pleasing, but very lasting manner.

13 July: New Moon in Cancer

You finally got the hang of it – I mean, what constitutes true success. You realize, like I did long ago, I must confess, that it comes from getting the most out of life. Not necessarily in money or material terms. You will give the best of yourself to both family and profession. And in doing so, make the best use of your time, energy, resources. There is a freshness in your methods that brings joy to the most mundane of tasks.

19 July: First Quarter in Libra

You are in the frame of mind now that makes you want to assess, evaluate, even calculate your own achievements. These could be external or inner growth. A new, responsible *you* emerges, even diplomatic but more outgoing, more caring. Perhaps these are new heights of excellence or achievement, after all. Assignment, commitments, projects are successfully dealt with now.

27 July: Full Moon in Aquarius

The theme will definitely be ties. The growth you have experienced within you over the last weeks sets your feet firmly on the road to new bonds and ties – of love, of duty, of family, or of legal ties at work. You will need to be flexible, adaptable, open, in order to make them work – both at home and at the workplace. You'll do brilliantly at creative pursuits like the arts, music and theatre, a touch of drama, in speculation and investment, hobbies and even cinema and the media.

4 August: Last Quarter in Taurus

There is a danger of pursuing wrong career objective, even being irresponsible in your approach to work. The reason could be some anxiety, neurosis, niggling ailments, feeling out of sorts, which could tempt you to make the wrong moves now. The highlights will be passion and sex, loans and funds, and paradoxically, religion and spirituality.

11 August: New Moon in Leo

It's the right time, perhaps even the best time for family and social activities, even perhaps so much of the latter that you could neglect dear ones and well-wishers. Old and new friends will be important. You are outgoing, friendly, classy, amiable. It's the ideal time to ask for favours. The success rate will be high, but you'll have to respond similarly when it's necessary to help others. Nothing comes for free.

18 August: First Quarter in Scorpio

You'll be doing two things that will make life smoother right now, and also augur well for the future. On the one hand, entertaining, friends, social gatherings; and on the other, a revamp or overhaul of finances and career/profession. There will be risks of spending too much on business concerns, in an attempt to raise your income.

26 August: Full Moon in Pisces

Ganesha now impels you to a bout of introspection. You could also be strongly into healing, succouring, nursing those who need it. In the process, of course, you will yourself be healed and helped out of the angst, neuroses that could overcome you. Self-analysis will draw you more than material concerns; also charitable work, welfare concerns. It's you as part of the larger community that is stressed now by Ganesha.

3 September: Last Quarter in Gemini

Philosophical pursuits, questions of law and order, social justice, research, the environment will keep you drawn towards them. Travel will be a release and a learning experience too. There will be visits, meetings, interviews, conferences and publicity too. Interfacing with people is the keynote, be it collaborations or networking in a larger framework, or even just in-laws and both near and distant relatives.

9 September: New Moon in Virgo

The introspective life, the passions of the mind once again. The monthly trend continues. Insights into life, cosmic questions, karmic laws, psychology. Once again, welfare, charity, healing and helping will keep you very busy. There may be a tendency in all this to dream up troubles, or try and carry the world's problems on your shoulders.

16 September: First Quarter in Sagittarius

You will now be in the mood to break new horizons, get a new slant on life. The unique, the different, always hold an attraction for Librans in their quest for harmony. Travel and information technology will be interesting for you, especially the Net. Don't be too proud to ask for help, when needed. Also important are trips and ties with neighbours, relatives, friends.

25 September: Full Moon in Aries

Your mind is fixed on gentler paths, and your mood more mellow, romantic and affectionate. Travel for pleasure or work, renewal of old partnerships or forming fresh ones, romantic ties and attachments too, perhaps leading up to marriage, will be in the focus. So, trips and ties could sum it up best, and it's a trend for the coming birth month as well.

2 October: Last Quarter in Cancer

You will suddenly be like a nuclear powerhouse in terms of both energy levels and activity. The astrological reason,

besides it being your birth month, is the long-range effect of
the planets. You will be dynamic, setting a punishing pace,
meeting targets, deadlines, achieving seemingly impossible
height of energy and power!

9 October: New Moon in Libra

In your birth month, with the charge of energy you seem to
have miraculously received, you will not only look at the
brighter side of things but also have much to be cheerful and
excited about. The worst of your troubles will be over. Your
attitude will attract success and achievement. You brighten
up your life, more practically, with a mint-fresh new look,
image, clothes. Positive thinking indeed, chuckles Ganesha.

16 October: First Quarter in Capricorn

House and home and domesticity have never seemed more
pleasant to you. You love them, warts and all (I mean
squabbles, hang-ups as well as fun times and joys). All the
same, you'll be working more than hard, sights firmly fixed on
where you plan to get. The energy for it has already come to
you. Your stars say that you will really make things happen!

24 October: Full Moon in Taurus

All this and heaven too could well be the theme for the
coming period. Flights of fancy, the supernatural, the
esoteric, the metaphysical, life after death, the deeper
meaning of life all possess your mind and intellect, now that
the worries of day-to-day life are behind you. On this topic,
let me just say that in addition to any or all of the above,
financial matters will have to be dealt with – loans, funds,
buying and selling, capital, joint finances, investments – any
or all, once again.

31 October: Last Quarter in Leo

Once again, a total shift. It's not that you are weak-minded, vacillating between different ideas, but it's just that your sheer mental energy has to let off steam; in addition to it there's your thirst for knowledge and wisdom. It's excitement of a totally different kind now – relaxation, fun and games, recreation, partying and dancing the night away. There will be greater closeness and intimacy too with the special person(s) in your life, in your serious look at the lighter side of life!

7 November: New Moon in Scorpio

Financial matters will need both considering and attention. Taxes, additional income, revenues and rentals, family funds. Also, improving or acquiring property and assets. On the personal level, relationships will be supportive with much mutual give and take. Your outlook and environment both change and others will be cooperative and sharing, bowled over by your charm!

15 November: First Quarter in Aquarius

Getting things will be important. Also, relationships full of reciprocity, love, warmth. You will be cherished, treasured, especially in terms of bonding with children. Approaching nuptials too, yours or of someone very close to you. Yet again, plenty of physical activity, fitness regimes, sports and exercise so that you're on your toes both literally and figuratively.

23 November: Full Moon in Gemini

You will have finally arrived – in terms of achieving the goals you set yourself, in terms of social status, financial security, bonds and relationships. All the activities undertaken between July to September bear fruit, yield dividends now. Ganesha adds a warning: No resting on your laurels, please. Reach out for all that had evaded you, and make definite plans for the future. It's necessary.

30 November: Last Quarter in Virgo

There is much prestige, power and glory for you, but you're also possessed by a dangerous kind of restlessness. This will need to be kept in check. You will be drawn to occult and arcane practices, a study of tantric precepts, of getting the cosmic energy generated by an awakened kundalini, for example. Know where to draw the line. Have adoration, but also submission to your Lord, your maker.

7 December: New Moon in Sagittarius

Perhaps you heeded my advice, as always, inspired by Ganesha. Who else? I submit totally and unconditionally to him. Anyhow, you will be busy building up contacts, not out of necessity or a desire for social climbing but for the sheer joy of it. Librans need human warmth, interaction, relationships. You will be involved with creative pursuits, particularly music and poetry, the arts, and specially the electronic media, like graphic designing, desktop publishing.

15 December: First Quarter in Pisces

There will be another charge of energy for you, albeit a gentler one. It gives you the sheer energy, vigour and 'go' to once again work hard and spectacularly achieve the most wonderful of results. The results will really be spectacular, but in restrained, quieter, definitely more personal way. By spectacular, I'm using the literal meaning – worth watching!

22 December: Full Moon in Cancer

The year 2018 draws to a close with a trendsetting quarter, where the millennium is concerned, for Librans. I have pointed out elsewhere, in several articles in fact, but do it again here, that the new millennium actually starts from 2019. Nothing will seem unattainable. You can reach out and touch the stars. Despite these heights seeming to be dizzying, you will have what it takes – the capacity to work at full strength.

29 December: Last Quarter in Libra

Once again, money, money and more money will be your focus – rentals, taxes, investments, trade and commerce, capital formation. These will all be favoured – also publicity and communications – both the spoken and the written word, ads and campaigns, friends and acquaintances, some romantic interludes, some gains in terms of pleasure.

SCORPIO

23 October–22 November

Ganesha wants me to take the symbol of the eye for Scorpios. Scorpio is the investigative eye, the hawk's eyes, the all-seeing eye, and the bionic eye of modern technology. In addition, the Italians say, *'L'occhio vuole sua parta'* (or, the eye demands its share).

- **Element:** Water
- **Ruling planet:** Pluto
- **Co-ruling planet:** Mars
- **Quality:** Fixed (=stability)
- **Quality most needed for balance:** A wider view of things
- **Day:** Tuesday
- **Gems:** Bloodstone, malachite, topaz
- **Metals:** Iron, radium, steel, plutonium
- **Scents:** Cherry blossom, coconut, sandalwood
- **Colours:** Dark red, maroon, crimson and the colours of smoky cloud formations

- **Cities:** New Orleans, Cincinnati, Washington DC, Newcastle, Valencia and Liverpool
- **Number:** Nine
- **Flowers:** Red chrysanthemum, red carnation, rhododendron, honeysuckle, gentian

Special Message from Bejan and Nastur: In ancient times Virgo, Libra and Scorpio were one sign. My special observation is that all these three signs are very choosy and fussy about food and health and may have phobias. I repeat that they *may* have phobias. I do not say that all of them have definite phobias. I have noticed that you Scorpios are the most intense of all the signs. In other words, you can hate and love with powerful passions.

JUPITER

Jupiter will be in your own sun sign from 10 October 2017 to 8 November 2018. Here Jupiter is at its brilliant best. Ganesha says this is what Jupiter will do for you. You will motivate, inspire and work tirelessly for the world in every possible way. The reason is Jupiter, the planet of plenty and prosperity, will be in your own sign by Western astrology. Jupiter means hope, love, creativity, power, pelf, prosperity, plenty of goodies and finally spirituality.

Scorpio is personality plus. Therefore, you must be up close and personal with people and thus influence them. Make the first move. Do not be selfish. Control your pride. Start new work. You will not only impress but guide others. Here is your big chance. Don't blow it. In the language of cricket, have patience, hit the loose balls and score a much-needed century. In women talk, have the perfect facial and make-up and the best lotion and cream in the world for the glow on your skin. I am sure you have now got what I am trying to say.

SATURN

By Western astrology, Saturn will be in your third angle from 21 December 2017 to 22 March 2020. This is a really tricky and unpredictable placing. The third angle symbolizes daring, guts, mental competitiveness. The third angle also represents brothers and sisters, relationships as such, communication by all new-fangled and/or practical means, for example, computers, Internet, mobile, WhatsApp, email, i-cloud, fax, video calls, TV ads, YouTube ads, Instagram and so on. But do take your own time before deciding a major issue. Also, get the cooperation of neighbours and family, if possible. It will help psychologically and emotionally. July and November bring you rich rewards and recognition.

But Saturn has a flip side or other side. Saturn is a cool customer. Saturn is not emotional. Saturn is realistic and sometimes very hard on others. This is not the fault of Saturn. This is just the way Saturn is made. In addition, Saturn means duty and responsibility. There is a very wise saying, 'the kind cruelty of the surgeon's knife'. It is kind because it finally cures. It is cruel because it cuts through the skin causing pain. In other words, you may expect mixed results. Most possibly Saturn will work in your favour. But sometimes you will be frustrated, your hopes may not be realized, your children may give you both joy and sorrow. Your endeavours and ventures will be thwarted or stopped for some time. My solution is very simple. Patience and perseverance will see you through. Finally, there will be sunshine. Why? The astrological reason is Jupiter the planet of good luck and Saturn the stern task master are luckily and powerfully placed in 2018. That is the key.

Mars by old astrology is your main planet. Mars will be in your own sign from 1 to 26 January 2018, and this will give you a head start. In other words, you will kick off or start the year wonderfully well. It is action time. From 18 March to 15 May the goodies and the freebies and the sweets of life, love, luck and romance will be there for you. This will be repeated from 13 August to 10 September because Mars will be in your lucky third angle. Finally, the period from 16 November to 31 December will be the crowning glory of 2018. The simple reason is most of your wishes will be fulfilled.

URANUS

On and after 4 March 2019 Uranus moves outside your eighth angle. This is the last year Uranus will be in your angle of finance, loans, bad health, secret and open enemies, and all secretive deals of finance and romance. A little extra care and caution are the answer.

NEPTUNE

Neptune is very favourably placed with Jupiter in your own sign, therefore by your creativity and good luck you will win the day. All those who are artistic and creative will perform superbly. Engineering, architecture, constructing is also as creative as the fine arts. Leap forward and be victorious. But please avoid overindulgence of pleasure, drinks, drugs, food as these will lead to later complications. The word *gourmet* means a connoisseur of good food. The word *gourmand*, though having a similar meaning, is more often used to mean a person who enjoys eating and often overeats. Would you like to be a gourmet or gourmand or both? I leave it to you.

PLUTO

By modern Western astrology, your chief executive officer (CEO) is Pluto. Pluto couples with Saturn in your third angle, making you much more intelligent, sharp, clever, cunning, scheming, plotting and succeeding in touching the lives of many people in all possible ways. In other words, in 2018 you become the media expert of the entire world. This is a very bold prediction. Ganesha says it is true. You will have much to do with brothers and sisters, journeys and contacts, and contracts and communication in general.

MONTHLY ROUND-UPS

January: You will begin on a positive, winning streak, and journeys, ceremonies, good relationships should be the happy events; **February:** Changes on the work and personal frontiers will start and they have to be tackled with tact and skill; **March:** Socializing and friendship and gains, and a wish-fulfilment; **April:** Expenses, secret deals, looking after the sick and the needy; also you must safeguard your health; **May:** A progressive, go-ahead month as pointed out in the preceding forecasts for the planets; **June:** Finances, food, family, contracts and comforts; **July:** Meditation, the domestic scene, renovation and decoration, excellent rapport with people; travel and communication will be highlighted; **August:** Home, house, family, immigration, buying/selling/renovation; **September:** You're on top of any situation, and children, hobbies and creativity are emphasized; **October:** Job, health, pets, projects, colleagues and your relationship with subordinates and servants; **November**: Love/hate, cooperation/competition, collaboration/separation, trips and ties, signing of documents and drafts; **December**: Loans, funds, capital formation, buying/selling; do take care of your health and lowered vitality.

HAPPINESS QUOTA: 87 per cent

WEEKLY REVIEW (BY PHASES OF THE MOON)

2 January: Full Moon in Cancer

You're off and away to a fine start, in the Derby race of life itself. Hard work, undoubtedly so, but what can one achieve without it? And Scorpios are achievers. There will be a shooting upward in the graph of not less than five Ps: prestige, pelf, power, property and most importantly, personal relationships. Of this last you realize the true worth right now. House and property, new business deals, successful partnerships – all keep you both busy and happy.

8 January: Last Quarter in Libra

Hard work, dedication, meticulous attention to detail will all be the need of the hour. And you Scorpios are no strangers to these. They are, in fact, your meat and drink. I can sum up the forecast as new beginnings and the efforts they take to happen. Achievements in personal life will be all-important, rather than in the material sense.

17 January: New Moon in Capricorn

A spirit of daring, the willingness to take chances, to gamble with life itself, courage in your emotional life will be yours now. You will search for new links with the world: business, higher study and research, new means of earning. Don't get carried away and risk your neck in foolish acts of physical or financial daring. That way lies mortal danger.

24 January: First Quarter in Taurus

You feel a need, a compulsion, in fact, to have meaningful interaction with people and truly communicate with them, so that the relationships that may develop through this can truly be enduring ones. New places and people will be important, and, as a necessary corollary, travel. There will be an overall expansion and growth trend, in your personality, relationships, and, of course your job/work/profession.

31 January: Full Moon in Leo

A whole host of interests and commitments form the trend for this period. Joyful romance, family life, spiritual pursuits, even community welfare and social issues on the mental and emotional fronts. In finance, it will be property, inheritances, will and codicil, money from home. The influence of your heredity and parentage will be important in all you do.

7 February: Last Quarter in Scorpio

You will need financing for your plans for the future, whatever they may be. You'll want to earn them yourself, so hard work is bound to be very much there. Also, family pressures, demands, commitments. To make life that much sweeter, there are amusements, a round of parties, wining and dining, enjoyment of outings and even sport, if so inclined. Ganesha has dished out a lot of variety on your platter.

15 February: New Moon in Aquarius

It's time now for some ease, some repose after the punishing pace at which you've been working. There will be time for social gatherings and parties, entertainment, amusement, and, most importantly, romance and affair of the heart: warming love. Also, your children, your own hobbies, creative arts. You will realize that life is not all work, though the rewards of work like promotions, benefits, bonuses are there too.

23 February: First Quarter in Gemini

Both work and play will lose some of their charm for you, even though you may go through the motions. It's time for religion, prayer, meditation, all forms of spiritualism that may appeal to you. You will shift to a level other than the worldly, material one, and these new values, including social, environmental and idealistic concerns, will be all-important. Ganesha draws you to himself.

2 March: Full Moon in Virgo

Expenses will threaten to go through the ceiling, but so will your income grow to match, so you will cope rather well. There could be success at business, the launch of new ventures or campaigns, to add to your confidence. There's also much socializing, party hopping, family outings, trips and visit so you're having a good time on several fronts. Your concerns with welfare, social issues, community projects will also keep pace, so all in all a busy and productive phase.

9 March: Last Quarter in Sagittarius

You'll function at two levels, once again. In this world, it's house and domestic concerns, office routines and demands, business commitments that will be important; while in the world of higher consciousness, you are contemplative, introspective, meditative. And the beauty of it is that both mesh wonderfully! There could be some jealousy, hard feelings or rivalry to cope with, but everything can't always be rosy, can it now?

17 March: New Moon in Pisces

You'll be very much a part of the mundane world with all its joys and sorrows, trials and compensations. In fact, you laugh, have a good time and enjoy life with the best of them. At the same time, your love affair with philosophy, religion, social and moral values and concerns continues to enthral you like a lady-love. You will function efficiently and happily on two planes and enjoy both, benefit from both.

24 March: First Quarter in Cancer

In your analytical and thoughtful frame of mind, you will try to identify and do away with the hindrance to your progress. Private and confidential matters, secret concerns will be important. There may be a house/office switch or even a change of job/profession. Your lifestyle will certainly change, becoming quieter, less flashy – economies at the office and the home too. This last could create some bad vibes, some hurt feelings.

31 March: Full Moon in Libra

A troubled phase is in store for you now. Don't get disheartened when I go into the details; remember Ella W. Wilcox's poem about the joys and sorrows of life, where she realizes 'This too shall pass away'. To get down to brass tacks: expenses and worries will skyrocket, work will be demanding, difficult and tricky, and someone might just let you down.

8 April: Last Quarter in Capricorn

Your home and domestic matters make great demands on you and you'll have to be slogging hard at the workplace too. There could be problems, hold-ups and delays too, health problems for yourself, your dependents, pets and extra attention required for home affairs. Group and team activities will almost knock you out. Learning to cope will be an exercise in self-restraint and determination.

16 April: New Moon in Aries

You'll be fighting the clock, struggling to get things done, meet deadlines. Expenses will be heavy, but you'll meet them too. Trusts, legal issues, inheritance and property, partnerships and collaborations, ties with loved ones and family – all clamour for your attention, time, effort. With superhuman effort, you will do all that's required of you, and more. Ganesha advises you to do it gracefully.

22 April: First Quarter in Leo

Worries and troubles will continue. I'm not being a prophet of doom. These phases come to all of us. The important thing is: a) deal with them with dignity, grace, restraint and; b) realize that nothing lasts forever, not even bad times. Things will change but it will be a slow process. By the end of the period, and certainly after mid-May, there will be personal gain, financial ease, social interaction. At last, say you and Ganesha!

30 April: Full Moon in Scorpio

A change in your fortune finally, you will think. Worries, doubts and uncertainties will ease, legal cases, contracts, deeds will be taken care of, prospects for future gain from business will be visible now. Also, a fair amount of wining and dining, extending and receiving hospitability, guests and family interaction. A different and very welcome trend for the period to come.

8 May: Last Quarter in Aquarius

You will get much joy, fulfilment, satisfaction from two of the best possible sources: a) your family and loved ones, and b) your own creative talents and abilities. Socializing, hospitality, parties will continue too. Finances will ease in the sense that your income will stretch to meet the many demands on it, so there's no shortfall at all. So, it's the three Fs of food, family, finance wherein you see this marvellous improvement.

15 May: New Moon in Taurus

A sudden somersault in your values. Your family, personal values, social duty and commitments are all important. Your public image will improve, also your credit and worth. Pending matters which have nagged at you, and caused anxiety and tension to you and the family will get sorted out. Try to be amicable in doing this. Any aggression that you display now could have harmful effects on you later in the year.

22 May: First Quarter in Virgo

Both financial and spiritual activity will be speeded up. Your mental and spiritual strength will see you managing finances, fund-raising, capital formation and management with more restraint and good sense. Sometimes you will see a slowdown in progress, but right now, perhaps 'haste makes waste' would have applied to you; so perhaps it's a good thing, after all, says Ganesha.

29 May: Full Moon in Sagittarius

You will need grit and determination as delays, chaos, problems have to be dealt with. Strenuous activity, health problems, perhaps hospitalization will all take their toll. Money matters will need not just your attention, but skill and enterprise as well, since they'll be majorly important, even vital. I must warn you once again to safeguard your health and not tax yourself too much.

6 June: Last Quarter in Pisces

You will find that there is a let-up in your anxieties. A possibility of fulfilling an ambition will appear. Personal relationships, family affairs, secret matters, confidential deals, or tax and legal matters will all have to be dealt with. But perhaps you will be able to see the light at the end of the tunnel, or at least the direction in which to go in the future. Ganesha has relented and decided to hold your hand.

13 June: New Moon in Gemini

Domestic responsibilities and care have to be honoured, especially as a parent or a spouse. The family will be the basis of your social life too, but you will still have to fulfil all the demands it makes on you, time- and money- wise. The pace at work will be rather hectic, and demanding too. Meet all these demands with composure, pleasantness, dignity. That way you gain from it.

20 June: First Quarter in Virgo

At last you will feel that your goals can be achieved, so that you can afford to relax, take things a little easy, party and enjoy yourself, interact with people. You will also have realized that too much of stress and strain take their toll, so you will balance work with recreation. That way you will learn to appreciate and enjoy both. After all, there are no absolutes – either all work or all play have both to be avoided.

28 June: Full Moon in Capricorn

You will travel and also change direction both at work and at home. The underlying reason will be a certain dissatisfaction with your lot, a restlessness that possesses you. Positive results will come from a course of study, research, new subjects, spiritual pursuits. All this will give you greater mental balance, inner harmony, peace of mind and relaxation. Your relationships benefit too, as you are more loving, caring and affectionate. What a wonderful trend for the month!

6 July: Last Quarter in Aries

You're a regular Friday's child, all through July, 'loving and giving'. The giving may take concrete form as in financial and material help, maybe a willing ear to someone's problems, supportiveness, care and comfort. It is these intangibles that add not only to your feeling of self-worth, but also this will continue through the month, at least, and come from loved ones, friends, parents, even neighbours and the community.

13 July: New Moon in Cancer

All the trends listed above will prevail in this phase too. In addition, the full moon makes you 'shop till you drop': (a kind of lunacy, isn't it?) for new clothes, cosmetics, accessories, jewellery, gadgets, music. There is, however, a method in your madness. The idea is the desire to improve your own self-esteem, enjoy life, add on the 'feel good' factor to it.

19 July: First Quarter in Libra

In this moon, you turn to your own motives, values, achievements, to assess them and see if you can improve them, so that you get what you want out of life. Family and home will be your priority, for life. Therefore, care of elders, pets, children, dependents comes automatically into the picture. Also family finances, marital funds and settlements, trusts, shared property, in order to provide comfort and security for those you love.

27 July: Full Moon in Aquarius

It's not people and places, as I'm fond of saying, but people, special people, those that make a mighty difference not just to your capacity to earn but also a huge difference to your emotions. There is the strong theme of romance and true love. In addition, communication with those in the media. This will not only change many of your perceptions but also add to your income. In fact, so also will the money and varied interests that you will now display.

4 August: Last Quarter in Taurus

Finance, passion and sex, but above all, spiritual advancement, tantra, mantra, ceremonies, rites and religion – quite a mix. Paradoxically, despite this plethora of interests/activities, a certain kind of depression/emotional weariness/restlessness too. It may even drive you into carelessness with regard to the kind of financial deals you cut – not shady so much as risky. Remember, there are no short cuts in life, or in astrology either!

11 August: New Moon in Leo

Both your expenses and your home/office responsibilities

will register a really sharp rise. All this is bound to make terrific demands on your time and energy. It's a testing time for you when the right values and the right attitudes not only bring you the deserved rewards, but much personal joy as well. You could perhaps have been feeling, for some time now, that you are neither appreciated nor given your just dues.

18 August: First Quarter in Scorpio

Two great benefits come to you in this phase. Both difficult to measure, but wonderful to experience. One will be that your spiritual life and energies enable you to be much more caring, warm, loving, accepting of attitude. Perhaps as a corollary of this, you will be able to gain much rest, relaxation, enjoyment of life. There will be a touch of class, style, graciousness in all that you do.

26 August: Full Moon in Pisces

Foundations of major, even mega differences in: a) finances, b) recognition, fame, achievements and c) most importantly, a far better quality of home life. It won't all drop into your lap from the heavens. Foundations need a lot of hard work, digging deep enough. New projects and financial matters will have to be planned for, and dealt with very carefully indeed, but plaudits and glory will be the outcome. Also, a burst of energy, confidence and faith in yourself and in the future. Ganesha's generosity is marvellous.

3 September: Last quarter in Gemini

This week will make you think that I don't know the first thing about astrology, or forecasting. All your worries, tensions will seem to resurface and you'll wonder just what

I was talking about in last week's forecast. A huge workload and ceremonies, public dealing, conventions and campaigns add to it. So too do construction, repairs, extensions, renovation to your house/home. You'll have to work all the hours God made, but He assures me that He rewards those whose faith remains unshaken, fixed on Him.

9 September: New Moon in Virgo

A kind of calm, the 'peace that passeth all understanding' descends on you. A good, powerful positioning that will work miracles for some. The benefits: meditation, prayer, religious rites leading to joy and tranquillity. Better harmony at work, and on the domestic scene. Efficiency will soar, so too will achievements, naturally, over time. You reach out to help those more needy, more sick, more infirm, more sorrowing, than you.

16 September: First Quarter in Sagittarius

A time for your creative talents, original thinking, skills and enterprise will shine. Also your children and their talents. A strong desire to assert yourself and stand up to demand your rights, also a keen interest in the new, the mysterious and the esoteric – in life, and in human knowledge. All to the good, of course, but you can attain your own hopes/expectations/ ambitions without trampling on others.

25 September: Full Moon in Aries

Popularity, warmth and caring, wish-fulfilment, the realization of hopes and dreams for the future; now is the hour, or rather moon's quarter for all this to come to pass. Parties, outings, family ceremonies and gatherings – all full

of fun and laughter, glitter and joy. Strong family bonding too, though there are some conflicts. There always are, but you keep your temper and the family circle intact. A truly wonderful trend for October.

2 October: Last Quarter in Cancer

Once again, the same determination, confidence, energy that you experienced end-August. Tremendous efforts are easily made to accomplish all you set out to do: targets and deadlines, achievements and assignments. You work, play, love and are loved with equal intensity. The 'feel-good' factor is very, very high indeed, so also the praise that is lavished on you. Ganesha smiles. He enjoys it as much as you do!

9 October: New Moon in Libra

It's time for you to be busy with plans, philosophic thoughts, assessments of self and evaluation. Your optimism and confidence will affect your friends and family, your work and play, associates and superiors. Your image in the eyes of the world and in your own eyes too has never been better. You feel that this is where you've wanted to be, for a long time now. But there is humility, not pride, thankfulness, not self-congratulation in your attitude.

16 October: First Quarter in Capricorn

A thorough overhaul of family finances and your home is what you embark on now. Luxuries, gadgets, even objets d'art for your home – to improve the quality of life therein. An extra effort is naturally required but you'll do it with a smile on your face and joy in your heart. You'll be willing to go that extra mile, take that extra risk/gamble, sure that Ganesha will not let you come to any harm.

24 October: Full Moon in Taurus

You'll deal with the problems and pursuits of day-to-day life in this material world, but you'll have a secret life in the higher world running parallel. Rebirth and reincarnation, karmic death, psychology, extrasensory perception, the occult and the life hereafter will have a hold over your mind. Strongly, though, the trend is for love and laughter, a wedding or engagement, creative pursuits and hobbies. Also gambles, speculation, money-spinning deals.

31 October: Last Quarter in Leo

Family ties, romance, love and your own health register a major upswing, especially love, whether you're married or single. It's as if nothing can go wrong, and joy can have no end. Family finances, funds will have to be attended to, though so also will domestic matters. The bonding and closeness you experience makes all this very easy to handle, even pleasurable.

7 November: New Moon in Scorpio

All your efforts, no matter what they be, will meet with success. Your calm, peace of mind, mental poise are marvellous to behold. Of course, it all started with the new moon in Scorpio. But petty conflicts, problems will arise and so too will demands on you at work. Of course, again, you'll take them all in your stride, as confident and serene as perhaps Ganesha himself, who has made it all happen.

15 November: First Quarter in Aquarius

Work-related matters first: new ventures, partnerships and projects, are all revamped, streamlined by you. Now,

family, relatives, parents and in-laws, children and most importantly your loved one/spouse/mate draw into a magic circle of love and sharing. Finally, the community and society too will benefit from your care, attention, willingness to help, counsel, support. Perhaps you have never before been cherished and loved more than what you experience now.

23 November: Full Moon in Gemini

Profits and benefits: both materially and spiritually. Money matters first: joint funds, capital, loans, even household expenses will be dealt with, so that things go smoothly. Also legal issues, leases, legacies. Most importantly, a renewed faith in your maker, the desire to serve him sincerely in this work and the willingness to make the extra effort to do so. Religion, prayer, spirituality will be your mainstay in all you do.

30 November: Last Quarter in Virgo

Healthy rivalry and competition, good results, good publicity are focused. Teamwork and team spirit, group activity rather than trying to perform in solitary splendour will become important. Differences of opinion at the workplace will be reconciled very pleasantly, in the interests of the larger cause. You will be equally cooperative and understanding in settling squabbles in the family and/or disputes in the community or neighbourhood.

7 December: New Moon in Sagittarius

Communication is the name of the game, and possibly, contacts too. The last less important than the first. The whole world of website, the Net, information technology at its most sophisticated will be your scene now. Travel too will be a part of the action. A very profitable and pleasing time for those in the media, performing arts, literature, publishing. The results of your efforts should be truly spectacular.

15 December: First Quarter in Pisces

You'll have to deal with money matters at all levels, from the nitty-gritty of domestic expenses and funds to the higher, esoteric realm of finance/capital for projects, larger issues, profits, stocks and shares. Hard work, commensurate rewards will sum it up – financially and otherwise. 'Otherwise' will include a rise in status that is on the anvil now. However, the situation has to be studied carefully and approached with a healthy amount of caution. No scene of 'fools rushing in', please, warns Ganesha – ever wise, even watchful.

22 December: Full Moon in Cancer

You will accomplish much, achieve much acquire much too. These can even be valuables, priceless gems/antiques/artefacts/gold. Wealth in many forms comes to you in the millennium. The lode of gold includes a very large happiness percentage and tremendous spiritual gains. It's been a good year, in the last months, and the good news is that this was not a flash in the pan. Next year, Ganesha willing, promises to be even better. Raise your hands and say 'Hosanna'!

29 December: Last Quarter in Libra

Finances will be at the forefront, as there may be some rather drastic changes in your financial profile. You may find these a trifle unsettling, with your love of stability, but looking at the long-term benefits will not be too difficult. By the end of the month, though, philosophical issues will gain in importance and also the need to resolve a very personal issue like a wedding/engagement. A time to invest wisely which will lead to an increase in income, but not making a quick buck.

SAGITTARIUS

23 November–22 December

'After driver-less vehicles US wants talking cars to up road safety.' Typically, Sagittarians. Ganesha says speed, space, stars, spirituality are the four Ss for you, swift Sagittarians. Geminis and Sagittarians are the two speed kings of the zodiac. Both are multidimensional and very fast on the draw and the uptake. In 2019, yes 2019, Jupiter will come in the sign Sagittarius. The planet Jupiter in simple language belongs to the sign Sagittarius. Jupiter means all-round progress and prosperity. Therefore, the speed sign Sagittarius will get an extra thrust, boost, turbo power so to speak. Naturally, the world will be a mighty fast and speedy. The world will be ready to shoot to all the stars and beyond. The future is here, waiting, throbbing, and ready to be launched in a grand and unimaginable style.

- **Element:** Fire
- **Ruling planet:** Jupiter
- **Colours:** Blue, dark blue, violet, mauve, rich purple, red, indigo
- **Quality:** Mutability (=flexibility)

- **Day:** Thursday

- **Metal:** Tin

- **Scents:** Carnation, jasmine, myrrh

- **Rules:** Hips, thighs, lever and hepatic system; natural ruler of the ninth house

- **Qualities:** Mutability (Sagittarians are ambitious, even driven, generous, focused, freedom-loving, seekers of challenge, open to new ideas, innovation and exploration)

- **Gemstone:** Turquoise

- **Number:** Three

- **Flowers:** Narcissus, golden rod, pinks, pink carnation, dandelions

- **Foods:** Bulb vegetables such as onions, leeks and celery, currants, mulberries and bilberries; also sultanas (grapefruit is also attributed to Sagittarius)

Special Message from Bejan and Nastur: Cartoon king Walt Disney, chess grandmaster Viswanathan Anand, actors Raj Kapoor and Dilip Kumar, spiritualist master Osho are all Sagittarians. Comedy + Spirituality + philosophy + egotism + showmanship + astronomy + space research = Sagittarius. Fascinating fabric. Slightly lunatic.

Like Leos, Sagittarians think big; like Geminis and Aquarians, Sagittarians love travelling and possibly horse riding. In a word, Sagittarians shoot straight and hard for the future. My very personal observation is that the double-bodied sign Sagittarius stands for aviation, space, time, energy, black holes and the Milky Way.

JUPITER

Jupiter will be in your twelfth angle from 10 October 2017 to 8 November 2018. Visits to holy places, foreign lands, law-suits, accusations, suppressions and new unions are possible. You may have much to do with hospitals, centres of knowledge, wisdom, yoga, ashrams, welfare centres, meditation and charity. You could be initiated into secret knowledge and hidden mysteries, trusts, funds, finances and wills. But deaths and losses are also possible. However, expect more gains than losses. It is this unusual mix of pleasure and pain which makes the year unique for you! Yours is a dual sign, namely horse and archer. In 2018, you will be turning the searchlight within yourself. But by temperament and taste you are an extrovert. So, in 2018, you will be pulled in different directions. This will result in tremendous creativity, but you will not be at peace with yourself. My answer is do good, be brave and let goodness be your own reward. Yes, you can boast about it if you like!

SATURN

By Western astrology, Saturn will be in your second angle from 21 December 2017 to 22 March 2020. Please also understand, clearly and completely, that there are no guarantees, no sure shots, in life or in astrology. Robert Hand, my favourite astrologer, hands out this very important information to you: 'Now, as Saturn is in your second house, you have to learn what is really important to you, what you really value, this does not mean just material things, but also psychological, spiritual and moral values. In fact, these may take precedence over material values if that is where you need to work on self-understanding, try to avoid letting fear and financial insecurity run your life now, for this takes attention away from the task of restructuring your value system on the inner psychological level. The best course is to organize your finances as well as possible, so you don't have to pay much attention to them. If you get wrapped up in money matters, they will be a source of trouble.' Anything to do with buying and selling, wealth, speech (TV, radio, acting, events and so on), physical enjoyments, acquisition from father, food, taste, clothes, learning, anger, family members, servants will have mighty great importance for you in 2018. Quite a list!

URANUS

On and after 4 March 2019, Uranus moves outside your eighth angle. This is the last year Uranus will be in your angle of children, sports, creativity. Here sudden changes are possible. But it will hone up your skills and your talent will glisten as never before. Actor, artists and those in the liberal fine arts, as well as engineering, research and construction will do brilliantly.

NEPTUNE

Neptune floodlights your house, home, property, parents, in-laws, buildings in a happy way. Therefore, renovation and decoration, buying selling of property, jewellery, ships, huge expensive jets, weaponry, sports equipment are foretold. Anything to do with the sea will be pleasant and favourable and rewarding. What more do you want?

PLUTO

Pluto, the atom bomb planet, joins Saturn in your second house. The right time to make your presence felt in every possible way. At the same time, I have said that Jupiter in your twelfth angle will make you introvert and look within yourself. This is strictly speaking a contradiction in terms. But we human beings are very complex and contradictory. We can be so many different things at the same time. We are versatile and adaptable. Ganesha points out very clearly that this is the great secret of our survival, success and evolution. This is the master key of us humans.

MONTHLY ROUND-UPS

January: Legacy, finances, passion, but low vitality; **February**: Distant places, research, parents and in-laws, education, children, good fortune through meeting the right persons; **March**: Position, prestige, power, parents, home and property, rites and rituals for the living and the dead; **April**: Friendship, socializing, gains and glamour, realization of aspirations; **May**: Travel, restlessness, despite good fortune, expenses, care for health; **June**: Good going in terms of health, wealth and happiness, you should thank Ganesha for it; **July**: Finances, family, ties, adornment, home, buying/selling, vehicles; **August**: Contacts, communication, contracts, crash courses, mental brilliance, new projects, courage, determination; **September**: Home, family, treasure, parents and in-laws, work prospects even for the retired, paradoxically, elderly persons will retire shortly; **October**: Journey, ceremony, publicity, children, hobbies, creativity – therefore, a lively and lucky month; **November**: Job, pets, projects, care for subordinates' health; **December**: Love/hate, partnership/separation, but all told, you do gain and can look forward to the future with great confidence. You deserve it!

HAPPINESS QUOTA: 80 per cent

WEEKLY REVIEW (BY PHASES OF THE MOON)

2 January: Full Moon in Cancer

Ganesha says you start the millennium with the emphasis on house and property, home, family. There will be taxes to be paid, a budget to be worked out, but all in relation to acquiring, renovating or registration of a home, or a property. Your family and loved ones will seem to be part of you – or vice versa. It's your own image you see reflected in their actions, pursuits and work.

8 January: Last Quarter in Libra

Lady luck smiles at you this week. Family support, well-wishers and friends add to your feelings of self-confidence and security. You'll be lucky at both cards and love, at gambling in other ways, speculation. Success crowns any effort you choose to make. You're really on a roll, as the cricket commentators say, and it's a rollicking time you're having in the bargain. Underlying it will of course be hard work and determined pursuits of goals.

17 January: New Moon in Capricorn

Your focus now shifts to interactions with people at all levels. Your own attitudes will determine the quality of both personal and professional relationships now. You will need to generate and create confidence in other people who can help you in your own work/business. There will be much advancement for you this way. No man is an island, remember, not even a Sagittarian. Human relations and relationships are all-important for human beings.

24 January: First Quarter in Taurus

You will network, mesh, interact with others, but may be inclined to be touchy, imagining neglect or lack of attention. There will be love and romance in your life, fun and party hopping, social gatherings. Your own hobbies, interests, comforts and pleasures will be focused by you, and you will attach much importance to them. Needless to say, you will make an effort to raise the money to finance them. So, it's personal finances that will be important too.

31 January: Full Moon in Leo

The four Fs – family, funds, food and finances. I'll explain food – the rest are self-explanatory – it's not just being a glutton, or lover of food or gourmand, or even a gourmet, but entertaining, extending and accepting hospitality are all covered by this word. There will be some drastic financial changes that can suppress you a bit, but you're well and truly on the lookout for opportunities for earning, by making either a killing or a quick buck, luck permitting.

7 February: Last Quarter in Scorpio

Financial deals, even sharp ones, if necessary, will be the main focus. You need to feel financially secure and will go all out for it. Family solidarity will be important for the same reason – even the parent–child interaction, from either end of the equation – and also matters related to family and personal property.

15 February: New Moon in Aquarius

You'll be bold, daring, adventurous, in matters of the heart and in finance. Speculation will prove lucrative. Shifting your home or office may be likely. You'll be passionate, not just physically, but in your keen interest in tantra, mantra, religion, the spiritual and occult phenomena, soul life, pursuing them with the single-minded determination that is the hallmark of Sagittarians. It may lead you to thank Ganesha for his many kindnesses.

23 February: First Quarter in Gemini

Your family, personal assets, wealth, papers and deeds and documents all need much care. You'll need to use discretion and good judgement to sort out the angle of finance and income, as moneymaking prospects and travelling for work or business conferences, meetings and presentations will both increase sharply. You tend to go all out, overdoing things and overstraining yourself, which you must hold in check.

2 March: Full Moon in Virgo

This is a good period for you that is being initiated, in terms of a) personal possessions, b) home and family, c) children, parents, in-laws, loved ones. Some pending domestic matters will be resolved, and finances will be easy. No hassles on that score. So, avoid being argumentative, demanding unnecessary showdowns. Try to maintain the harmony and accord that Ganesha has so kindly given you.

9 March: Last Quarter in Sagittarius

Family and home once again. More particularly house and home. Renovation, acquiring gadgets, making extensions or repairs, or perhaps buying a home of your own. Perhaps a housewarming or *grihapravesh*. Also important will be your interaction with family at different levels, and with local and neighbourhood concerns and affairs.

17 March: New Moon in Pisces

The overall theme or motif will be communication. It will vary from intensely personal and physical contact to letters, faxes, emailing friends overseas, interaction with relatives and neighbours. Part of this will also be travel, or at least the making of travel plans. There will actually be a mental reaching out and expansion and all the above will be the forms it manifests itself in.

24 March: First Quarter in Cancer

Contacts and communications continue to be highlighted, along with group activity, in the pursuit of new ideas, new fields of study. Vital decisions should be thought over very carefully indeed, if they can't be postponed for the time being. You will show great intellectual capacity, optimism and vision in handling a new, experimental trend of activity, but you have to be careful that it doesn't turn negative for you.

31 March: Full Moon in Libra

Joyful relationships is the theme in this period most definitely so. It can be platonic friendship, acquaintances turning into friends or lovers, especially those who care. All this makes you relax your guard, let down your defences, get closer to people and, most importantly, love. You will, in turn, make less demands, be more tolerant and kind. Your health, mental attitudes and stance in life will all register an improvement.

8 April: Last Quarter in Capricorn

Ties, bonds, relationships – reaching out your hand in friendship, love and companionship to those around you. This departure from your usual self-contained Sagittarian identity is not just a blessing from Ganesha, it's your own changed perspective, where upbeat people rather than aggressive ones attract you more. Hard, intense work, much activity, yet time to laugh a little, love a lot. Travel too.

16 April: New Moon in Aries

Your travel may take on the ultimate, wider perspective of global, space or futuristic inter-planetary travel. Writing, research, higher studies, websites on the Net, lectures, exchange of learning and of ideas. Your inputs, to coin a phrase, will be both original and valuable in all spheres. Care while commuting and travelling, handling and signing documents, will all be necessary. Contracts and agreements too. You'll need to read the fine print many times over.

22 April: First Quarter in Leo

You will feel let down, both with your plans and with people, as neither will come up to your just expectations of them. Disillusionment is one of the sad facts of human existence. But Ganesha gives you an added spurt of willpower, self-confidence and common sense to rise to the challenge, pick up the gauntlet that life has thrown you and change everything to a more favourable bent.

30 April: Full Moon in Scorpio

You'll put out all the stops on the work front. The focus will be on intellectual activities, full of insight and vision for future gain and better relationships at the same time. You will be loyal, dedicated, steadfast in family bonds and matters, even if you need to trample on others, not just tread on their toes. There will be strain and tension in emotional attachments, children's issues, marital issues. You may feel imposed upon. Don't be too harsh in your dealings.

8 May: Last Quarter in Aquarius

Health may be suspect, after the physical and emotional strain you have been undergoing. You will need people at this time, so don't try to do things, solve problems all by yourself. A little recreation and relaxation, a shopping spree even if you can't afford it, won't come amiss. If you overextend yourself, there could be burnout or collapse. And that's counterproductive, isn't it, asks Ganesha.

15 May: New Moon in Taurus

Don't make any decisions in haste, or you could regret in leisure. The focus is almost totally on work, hard work without any thought of rewards. Ganesha assures me – and you – that they will come. Right now, once again, negativism and criticism of others must be avoided. You may need the support of others now, for your own welfare and to further your projects.

22 May: First Quarter in Virgo

Better health, better family bonding, more rest and relaxation. Sweetness and warmth in all relationships, not just personal ones, will make all this happen. It is a favourable time for starting up new projects and winding up pending matters to your satisfaction. Talking of satisfaction, it's your mind and intellect that gets the most in domestic, community and social concerns, larger global issues.

29 May: Full Moon in Sagittarius

You're once again focusing on both the family and the community where your attention, activity and care are concerned. You now see them as extensions of yourself and are ready to include them in your personal objectives, along with career and work. Travel is almost definite, though not without some delays or risks. These can be major or minor, but they're there in some form this period.

6 June: Last Quarter in Pisces

A quarter when you may feel that things are just getting to be too much for you. Matters concerning the problems of dependents/children will require sacrifice and effort on your part, before problems ease out. In your desire to help, and serve, you may have to stretch yourself to the limits, and beyond. Relaxation, unwinding a bit, are as necessary, says Ganesha, as commitment to duties and chores.

13 June: New Moon in Gemini

Let me use that old favourite of mine, 'trips and ties' – a phrase which sums up the major focus this week. Trips – travel for work, pleasure, even for love, pilgrimages, spiritual and intellectual journeys. Ties – family and marital bonds, but also partnerships, collaborations, mergers in business or at work. The risk of injury and trauma that was hinted at last week continues in this period too. Accidents too, or perhaps breakages and loss.

20 June: First Quarter in Virgo

Higher studies, faith, future aims and plans will hold your mind and attention. You might even take an examination or interview, join a course of study. Legal issues may be closed out, but don't take gambles in investing family resources, funds or even household ones. There could have been some confusion prevailing in your affairs which may be resolved around now. This could even have been a strictly personal matter.

28 June: Full Moon in Capricorn

Group activity, teamwork, interaction with friends and acquaintances, even for professional/business matters is where you're busy now. The theme or focus for the month to come is definitely and predominantly on funds, finances, money matters. You'll take on an extra workload and responsibilities and extra earning too. There may be a slight feeling of hurt or misunderstanding with your mate/spouse who may perceive a lack of cooperation on your part.

6 July: Last Quarter in Aries

You'll finally achieve a fine balance between home and work, professional demands and family affairs. A busy time, though, with finances, legal issues, love, romance, secret deals, family expenses, marital accounts, even gifts. You may even learn the knack of saving your energy and your money. There may even be a new source of income or avenue of gain. A good phase coming in from Ganesha, if you make the right choices.

13 July: New Moon in Cancer

New ventures will meet with success now. You will have

to learn to a) keep your own counsel in personal and professional dealings; b) keep your assets and plans under wraps; and c) avoid too much confidence in others regarding sharing of profits. You must be discreet, even guarded in your talk, correct both your aims and your strategies to achieve them. Get rid of negative ideas and thoughts. You will be the gainer!

19 July: First Quarter in Libra

Once again, your true nature, your profession and career objectives and thirdly, understanding and building bridges with your family will not only be important, but absolutely necessary. Astrology, the occult spiritualism, will be attractive, also discussions with people who share your interests and ideas. Right now, you'll have to think, plan, strategize!

27 July: Full Moon in Aquarius

Increments, gifts, a legacy or employment benefits will now be forthcoming. In that respect this week not only sets the trend, but is a continuation of the last. Better health and a fair amount of travel. Also, tremendous and deep interest in religion, faith, higher studies, future plans. A wonderful time for personal relationships ranging from friends, social gatherings, children and kin to romance and passion. They're all there – maybe even that one strong, enduring tie. Lucky you!

4 August: Last Quarter in Taurus

Travel, spiritual and intellectual growth, learning, study, wisdom; warmth, understanding and closeness in personal relationships; sharing of ideas and goals – doesn't this list sound like an existence in utopia? You will shun the limelight, be content to be a back-room boy (or girl), focus firmly on career and business without wanting the glory. Creative pursuits, children, love affairs may have some teething troubles, but then proceed smoothly, giving much joy!

11 August: New Moon in Leo

It's time for your 'people skills' to be put to the test. Parents, relatives, in-laws, partners, even correspondence will absorb you. Take care to do your homework, collect your data and inputs, before you enter into either discussions or commitments. Whatever you decide now vis-à-vis commitments will have a long-term impact and duration. It's, therefore, wiser to weigh your various options very carefully before you close out a deal, particularly with organizations or friends.

18 August: First Quarter in Scorpio

Planning ahead is necessary, in fact, vital, in this go-ahead month. A brilliant new overseas venture/enterprise may be initiated now. Domestic bliss will prevail, or harmony at the very least. Capital formation, loans and funds will click. You will perform miracles of achievement in both profession and caring for those you love. Recognition will come, along with a heightened self-esteem.

26 August: Full Moon in Pisces

Creative interests, quality time and interaction with children, social activity, entertainment and amusements, the company of friends and loved ones. They're all there for you with this full moon. Equally important – the quest for new ideas, long-term changes and commitments, maybe even lifelong ones. These can be professional or personal or even both. In certain respect, this phase oversees the total picture of you in the millennium, courtesy Ganesha.

3 September: Last Quarter in Gemini

A highly favourable, profitable and comfortable phase, with the moon in your Sagittarian quarter. I hope you'll agree that, if nothing else, I do have a way with words, the gift of the gab! Advancement in your job/career/profession/business will be partnered by gains in social prestige, clout, position. Hard work from you – but the rewards are there! Perhaps the best reward is the warmth, care, love, cosseting from everyone around you.

9 September: New Moon in Virgo

Your ambition and the desire to grow in your profession will be realized fairly soon, if not now. A lot of time and attention will be spent on a) both parental ties and duties to or as parents, and b) activities involving your superiors or those in the higher echelons of power. With all this, naturally, comes a rise in popularity and credit. Use tact and diplomacy in all your dealings.

16 September: First Quarter in Sagittarius

You want to get closer to people now, which is a uniquely different ball game. Sometimes it's difficult for Sagittarians to do this effectively, despite their deep need for it. It's inner growth you're after, having achieved the material gains that are more visible. You will explore and study your motives, impulses and inherent strengths to do so. A contemplative and thoughtful week from Ganesha. He really varies the 'different strokes' he uses.

25 September: Full Moon in Aries

A month of marvellous achievements in all spheres concludes now. It is now time to foster affection, bonds of care and trust, warm relationships. Your popularity will be tremendous. Also, the gains in terms of wisdom and the ability to assess your achievements. It's a time when you really feel you've got yourself a place in the sun.

2 October: Last Quarter in Cancer

Your success may well have gone to your head, since the popularity and authority you're enjoying right now is unparalleled. It may, therefore, incite you to invite trouble, buck the system, force showdowns unnecessarily, or just be rough in your dealings. Conflicts are bound to arise, but diplomatic handling and a soft approach can get equally good results. This applies to domestic squabbles, lovers' tiffs, marital problems too, which may arise about now. After all, that's what Ganesha does and he is worshipped as the remover of difficulties and obstacles – Vighneshwara.

9 October: New Moon in Libra

An additional surge of power and energy. This helps you not only to go from strength to strength in your job/profession, but also tackle and solve problems from the past. You'll learn management and negotiation techniques, maybe some other job-related skills. The focus, however, is on the domestic front this quarter – your duties as parent or child, responsibilities and attachment to home and hearth, even perhaps a home away from home. A wonderful sense of satisfaction is felt as a result.

16 October: First Quarter in Capricorn

Suddenly, you'll feel geared up for some tremendous strides in terms of progress – personal and professional. It's not a time for you to rely too heavily on others – could be some danger there! Yet, build bridges with people rather than fences. You'll realize that it's your own fears and inhibitions rather than outside influences that were slowing you down.

24 October: Full Moon in Taurus

The effect of the sextile will be felt more now. You will loosen up, have fun, be a party animal, flirt a little, love a lot. There will be a zing, a zest in all that you do, yet an inner reserve of rationality, internalization of all that you do. Conflicts may be experienced and there can be a showdown or two, but you know how to pursue your objective and make sure you achieve it. A certain strength of mind makes you rise above the fun and games.

31 October: Last Quarter in Leo

Introspection, evaluation of your aims and goals, even contemplation and meditation – a different kind of progress is made. It could all have been triggered off by a challenge on the work front. You'll also realize that the demands of your job/profession are a hindrance in your forming close bonds with others, much as you'd like to do so. These doubts are better handled with less stubbornness. You'll learn to deal with these contrary pulls, and in fact, resolve them for the greater good of all.

7 November: New Moon in Scorpio

Worry, nervousness, stress and tension are most unusual for you as a rule, Sagittarians. Yours is perhaps one of the most focused signs of the zodiac. But that's what you will experience and exhibit now. You will be drawn to solitude, quiet and lonely places, and also centres of healing and worship, religious shrines, courses in meditation, New Age thinking or in the art of living, as a release and relief. Travel is a strong likelihood, especially for this purpose.

15 November: First Quarter in Aquarius

Advanced ideas in religion, in the realm of the occult, will draw you and, in fact, become part of you. To such an extent that you feel you must share them with others. Love will truly warm the cockles of your heart now, become all-important with children. There can be minor differences that will be happily resolved, with this gentler persona of yours.

23 November: Full Moon in Gemini

A certain enlightenment of vision has been building up within you as your birth month approaches. It's a strong white light indeed, dispelling all despair and doubts. In fact, you may feel you're on your way to the realization of your fondest hopes and ambitions. Whatever, you will give – in the larger field or realm of altruism, philanthropy, charitable work – in the same mood, will you renew or contact old acquaintances and friends, make new ones, interact with family, kin, neighbours.

30 November: Last Quarter in Virgo

This change in outlook and attitude will colour all your activities in the month, and through to the new year. In addition, finances are spotlighted, but more in terms of major spending. You will be both friendly and sociable, networking and interacting with peop   in several different ways. All this means that you're spending heavily on social and business entertainment and activities. Career and finances will both need to be revamped in a big way.

7 December: New Moon in Sagittarius

Equal values, weightage and time will have to be given to both your career and your social activities. The pace will be truly hectic on both fronts. Action time now in terms of making major decisions, and coping with the huge serving on your platter of life – not just a slice of the pie. All doubts and hesitation will have to be done away with. You have to cause to move everything and everyone fast, hit every ball – googly, yorker, inswinger, outswinger, even one with a reverse swing – for a super six in the cricket match of life!

15 December: First Quarter in Pisces

Once again, much to do this week around. Your birth month is proving truly hectic – and that's wonderful. Never a dull moment! Behind-the-scene activities, a secret love affair, perhaps; most certainly romance, secretive, hush-hush deals, and also much partying and socializing! You'll want to outstrip everyone in the rat race, earn huge amounts of money, and yet score heavily in inner and spiritual growth too.

22 December: Full Moon in Cancer

You come full circle to the same quarter as at the beginning of 2018 – all set to go into the first year of the new millennium. Hard work, hard thinking, spectacular performance, and, of course, scintillating results and rewards! Family support, warm companionship from friends, gambler at high odds will pay off. You've struck pay dirt in the gold mine of life! Real estate inheritance, joint finance, collaborations will all thrive with your ongoing Midas touch, but personal relationships will not shrivel and die, as they did in the old fable.

29 December: Last Quarter in Libra

Associations formed around this time will be long-term ones. You will also learn to reconcile what your vocation is with your true nature. You will work out personal issues revolving around your career, identity and home. And it is at home that your heart is, this period. Your identification with both house and home will be very close, also with your parents, ancestors, going back to your roots in a fine show of genuine bonding.

CAPRICORN

23 December–22 January

Ganesha points out with his index finger that in Western astrology, the astrology of countries is called mundane astrology. By Western mundane astrology, India's main planet is Saturn. Saturn means ambition, mighty spirituality, old religions, Mother Nature, duty, responsibility. But Saturn also means very fixed old ideas, great difficulties in accepting change, fixed opinions and values, sometimes pettiness and miserliness, black money. This is nothing to be ashamed of. Human beings are a unique mix of the good and the bad and the in-between. Dhirubhai Ambani, Ratan Tata, Atal Bihari Vajpayee, Muhammad Ali Jinnah, Nawaz Shareef, Baba Kalyani, Salman Khan are all Capricorns. Saturn laughs in a sarcastic way.

Capricorns are level-headed, rational, born great managers and organizers, prefer order and regularity and want the world to work like a perfect machine. But they are smart enough to realize that the world is not exactly like that. This could frustrate them. But they have common sense. They finally learn to live with the world with all its faults, foibles and glories.

- **Quality:** Cardinal (= activity)
- **Day:** Saturday
- **Rules:** Knees, skin, and bones; natural ruler of the tenth house
- **Gemstone:** Garnet
- **Metal:** Lead
- **Colours:** Dark grey, dark green, black, dark brown and indigo
- **Cities:** Delhi, Mexico City, Ghent, Brussels, Oxford, Chicago and Montreal
- **Numbers:** Eight and two
- **Flowers:** Red poppy, pansy, red carnation, ivy
- **Foods:** Potatoes, beets, barley and malt, also starchy foods, onions, spinach and quinces

Special Message from Bejan and Nastur: My personal observation is Capricorns and Virgos are the ants, the workhorses of the zodiac. They like to be industrious, efficient, disciplined. I have seen that they are experts at management and organization. But I have also seen that they are better at managing and organizing others than their own selves. There is a very wise saying, 'In the affairs of others even fools are wise, in their own even sages err.' My dear Capricorn readers, please understand that I am only half serious and I do salute your industry, your efficiency and your capabilities. No hard feelings.

JUPITER

Jupiter will be in your lucky and exceptionally favourable eleventh angle from 10 October 2017 to 8 November 2018. The eleventh angle stands for all-round prosperity. Therefore, I would like to quote the Buddha: 'If we could see the miracle of a single flower clearly, our whole life would change.' In simple words, you will experience the miracle, the surge of life force itself. The joy of living, breathing, existing will be yours. Here are the other goodies of Jupiter for you: wish-fulfilment, group activities, financial gains, new opportunities for both pleasure and business (sounds good), awards and rewards, ancestral property, hidden treasures and so on. My advice is take the plunge for both profit and pleasure.

SATURN

By Western astrology, Saturn will be in your own sign from 21 December 2017 to 22 March 2020. There are two distinct sides to it: a) For you Capricorns, Saturn is the main planet, therefore you will be in tune with Mother Nature, spirituality, material possessions, food, taste, drinks, family; in other words, you will do things naturally. b) But the planet Saturn is by temperament harsh and demands discipline, duty, responsibility. All of us are human beings. We are a mix of the good, the bad and all that is in between. We are not perfect. We are still growing, still evolving. We have to put up with pain, misery, separation, bad health, disturbances. The main purpose of Saturn is most certainly to change your life in many possible ways. Most of us do not like change. We find it hard and difficult to adjust and adapt and adopt to changing circumstances, situations and the march of time.

So, for you Capricorns, Saturn could be a training process for the future.

In 2018, Saturn and Jupiter are in an excellent placing to each other. This will help you to move with the change and thus have the best of both the worlds. At least from time to time. And at other times you will come under the grip and grasp of a stern Saturn. Therefore, I would say mixed results but more in your favour.

Saturn is your main planet. But the other important planet I take for Capricorns is Venus. The first seventeen days, Venus will be in your sign and you will start the year in royal style. Go for it, as the Americans say. The period from 11 February to 6 March is for contacts and communication; 31 March to 24 April for creativity, children, sports, entertainment; 20 May to 13 June for sweet and sour relationships; 10 July to 6 August is for inspiration, imagination, pilgrimage, travel; September 9 to 31 October is best for drinking the cup of life to the very lees; 3 to 31 December is also for having a grand time.

URANUS

On and after 4 March 2019 Uranus moves outside your fourth angle of home, house, properties, parents, in-laws. Uranus usually disrupts and creates disturbances, but Uranus in modern terms is the terrorist. This terrorist will not trouble you on and after 4 March 2019. That's good news.

NEPTUNE

Neptune is like music in your life. You respond very well to music. A.R. Rhman is a Capricorn. Music will soothe you as well as inspire you. I suggest it is your elixir. You

Capricorns can also be great composers and poets, for example, Javed Akhtar.

PLUTO

Pluto embraces Saturn in your own sign and this will result in intensity of purpose, perhaps poor health but most certainly a tremendous drive to all your activities. Sometimes two opposite qualities rule and ride over the same person. Nothing in real life is all good and nothing in real life is all bad. Life is not black and white. It has many different colours or hues.

MONTHLY ROUND-UPS

January: Off and away to a magnificent start, despite pressures and pulls, says Ganesha; **February**: Windfalls, joint finance, legacy, passion; **March**: Right contacts, success, travel, publicity; **April**: Tremendous drive, ambition honed perfectly; **May**: Good news, pressures, delays, but all turns out well in the end, and do socialize; **June**: Expenses, losses, extrasensory perception and psychic powers, glimpses of Ganesha/God/Allah/the supreme power, pilgrimages, rites and duties; **July**: Success, happiness, fun and games, family, victory; **August**: Finances, family, the luck of the draw, buying/selling/investing; **September**: Fanning out to people, places, contracts and contacts, communications channels buzz; **October**: Home, house, in-laws, renovation/decoration in office/shop/home; **November**: Despite changes, you do enjoy yourself and are creative; children give joy; **December**: Work, health, loans, pets and projects.

HAPPINESS QUOTA: 83 per cent

WEEKLY REVIEW (BY PHASES OF THE MOON)

2 January: Full Moon in Cancer

Ganesha says it's contacts and communications for you, but on totally different, personalized level. Reaching out to the community, society, the world, in caring and sympathy; humanity at large is your family now. You feel that it's a better time by far – spiritually and emotionally. Better health, greater hope, greater confidence in yourself, despite recognition of your own limitations, all add up to a much, much higher percentage of both happiness and contentment.

8 January: Last Quarter in Libra

Self-esteem will show a rising graph, a feeling of being worthy. It will take material form in the a) care of property, lands, house or home – either acquiring if you haven't got them, or renovation, improvement and beautification; b) care of the elderly, particularly parents and in-laws. You are strong on filial and civic duty – humane and kind.

17 January: New Moon in Capricorn

This trend, initiated actually in January itself, with the stress on personal relationships, will now be firmly in place. In addition, though both professional and personal partnerships are emphasized, you will find most definitely that it's your relationships – all kinds, all levels – that make for a better and happier way of life for you. And that's mighty important.

24 January: First Quarter in Taurus

You've spent much effort and thought on putting your house in order – I mean this literally. Now you feel you can afford to relax, enjoy yourself, and also the good things of life. You'll be seen at parties, social gatherings, entertaining and being dined and feted. You'll be easy-going, full of fun and romance, pleasant and good to be with.

31 January: Full Moon in Leo

It's time to be more practical and level-headed in your approach, you realize. The 3 Fs are highlighted. Incidentally, food is for entertaining and hospitality, and funds for your income and expenditure. Finance implies the larger issue. Your pragmatic attitude and greater flexibility will now yield better results, both at home and at the workplace. You'll take care not to rub people up the wrong way, and will try to work together for shared goals.

7 February: Last Quarter in Scorpio

In finances, it will be stock market, brokerage, speculation that will be exciting for you. Don't get led up the garden path, though, by being too trusting of other people in your financial dealings. Also, make sure of the career objectives you decide to chase. Wrong moves can put more important things into serious trouble and danger.

15 February: New Moon in Aquarius

You are in the mood to take risks and chances, in your attitude to life particularly. Conservation and prudence are not for you now. It's like playing down the pitch instead of on the back foot – you go out to meet life halfway. Tantra and mantra, sex and passion, yet love and spirituality too. At any rate, there is an upbeat kind of restlessness about you now.

23 February: First Quarter in Gemini

Movement, motion, restlessness too, perhaps, might just about sum it up. Travel for both business and pleasure may happen. Spiralling expenses will have to be catered for, and alongside you will also cater to your deep need to expand your spheres of interest and anxiety. That's probably what's making you restless. There is a strong desire for swift and decisive action, a certain boldness of approach now.

2 March: Full Moon in Virgo

All the Cs – companions, contracts, correspondence, contacts, communication, collaborations. Group activities, social ties, reaching out from phone calls to Net chatting, even a chat with your neighbours over the garden fence – that's it for you this quarter and off and on throughout the coming month. For you, the millennium has truly turned the globe into a little village, where you want to know everyone.

9 March: Last Quarter in Sagittarius

It's your work/job/profession/business that you concentrate on almost totally, in a sudden shift. It's not inexplicable. The desire to transcend the merely physical is all-important and vital. It's not, however, a good time to make vital decisions, especially on the personal front. Even the demands of children and loved ones may seem to be bothersome.

17 March: New Moon in Pisces

Your own determination and faith in yourself will carry you through. It's not a difficult time, exactly: you'll just be a little short of funds, with too many demands on your purse and on your own creative abilities at work. It's not in you to muddle through anyhow, so you have to summon up immense reserves to cope with both.

24 March: First Quarter in Cancer

You're full of optimism, vision and hope once again. All your doubts and possible disheartenment are a thing of the past. You'll display tremendous mental capacity, rise above pettiness of any kind in both your professional and personal life. You don't even know what words like gossip, squabbles, arguments mean right now. Not only this, your own determination and imaginative thinking will be twice reinforced by your meeting and interaction with people who are compatible.

31 March: Full Moon in Libra

You turn to house and home, personal belonging, property as your primary focus. But it's different in approach to what your attitude was in the opening weeks of the year. Then too it was home and house, but now you will decide pending family matters, deal with relatives and kin, the neighbourhood and community, local and domestic affairs.

8 April: Last Quarter in Capricorn

You'll find yourself full of hope for long-term stability and future gain. It's the result of having put your house in order – both literally and figuratively – last week. You'll avoid personal hang-ups and issues in the larger interest. Strangely, though, there are chances of a second home or base, or a home away from home. You'll be out to revise your own individual position and foundations, in order to get what you want out of life.

16 April: New Moon in Aries

It's work and more work for you, now that you've got your sights firmly fixed on your goals and targets. You want to be an individual, stand on your own two feet, feel secure in your own right. That's true of both profession and finances. God made this happen. Naturally, health safeguards, adequate rest are a must, if you have to see it through.

22 April: First Quarter in Leo

You'll probably feel that you've never been so busy before, in your entire life. The main thing is, of course, the need to have a satisfactory income that keeps pace with your expenses. You'll be able to generate the income soon enough – the proper use of shared resources will ensure that – and you would finally get the hang of it. By shared resources is not necessarily meant family or marital funds. It could be friends, partners, collaborators.

30 April: Full Moon in Scorpio

Success will seem so close that you will feel you can reach out and touch it. Dreams and wishes may come true, perhaps in connection with someone or something truly near and dear like home, parents, family. All through the coming period the trend will be of achievement – that's something Capricorns are no strangers to. Some projects which you've had on the anvil for some time will now get started, with a flourish.

8 May: Last Quarter in Aquarius

Bonds and partnerships may now materialize, or, as I frequently like to put it – contacts leading to contracts. Thus, professional and personal life come together. It's human relationships – of all kinds and colours – that are the mainstay of all your activities now. There may be your own wedding, if still single, or that of someone very close to you as part of the bonds and partnerships scenario.

15 May: New Moon in Taurus

Very hard work indeed now, but there's the tremendous incentive of rewards for previous hard work to act as a spur. You're ready to do battle with the world, to carry on the metaphor. You're certainly riding home with the booty and loot, and feeling mighty thrilled about it. Promotions, bonus, ex-gratia payments, gain in finances and prestige, both important to trigger the 'feel-good' factor.

22 May: First Quarter in Virgo

You're not only in far better 'health and spirits' as we Indians say, but also have a lot going for you. Not least is just how charismatic and creative you are. Your inner resources will boggle even your mind, not to mention the capacity for slogging it out in terms of sheer hard work. All this will naturally put you not one step but yards ahead of the opposition. Way to go!

29 May: Full Moon in Sagittarius

Now that you have had an infusion of vigour, a recharge of batteries happening to you, in this new moon phase it's new interests, new possibilities, new avenues that will interest you. Hobbies and sports will be exciting, also your children's activities. Learning a new skill, higher studies, even research, if so inclined. Speculation and taking calculated risks too could be equally exciting.

6 June: Last Quarter in Pisces

You'll work hard, trying to give all your new ideas a concrete shape. Communication – both technology, and meeting and interacting with people – is not only strongly in focus, but will be the means to your ends. You'll be functioning at many different levels, so there could be a risk of burnout, stress, perhaps slight ill health. Problems of those kinds will prove to be a major setback for your plans.

13 June: New Moon in Gemini

Among the good things of life, you will definitely count love. Romance and falling in love are in the air. Also, travel and prosperity at enterprises. Alongside, expenses are on the rise. There is a slight risk of accidents or loss, so you'll need to be careful with your person as well as your purse. Don't go in for that risky deal or risky journey around this time, warns Ganesha.

20 June: First Quarter in Virgo

Personal and business concerns will have a tug of war for your time and attention. The signing of deeds and documents will be fairly important and there's the possibility of meeting just the right person – the one you've been looking for all your life. Social life, entertaining and entertainment too will find you willing to go all out.

28 June: Full Moon in Capricorn

Ties, particularly of marriage, will be the focus – your own, of your children or of someone equally close like siblings or relatives. There will be a lot to get through, both at work and in domestic matters, so you'll be kept on your toes. Acquisition of clothes and personal possessions too is strongly indicated. Skyrocketing expenses, of course, but maybe you're shopping for a trousseau or to set up your own little love nest!

6 July: Last Quarter in Aries

Professional and business partners will play an important role now, as you will have to come down to earth, tackle a load of hard work. An association for business is almost definite now, but you'll also have to contend with rivals and competitors, perhaps even in a court of law. At the same time both your public and private image in the eyes of those who matter will be vital, not just important.

13 July: New Moon in Cancer

Once again, the time is favourable for new ventures, enterprises, projects. You may get lucky and strike pay dirt. You'll be daring, willing to wrest both the initiative and the advantage. Actually, it's a different way of saying what I said, in the first sentence of this forecast, isn't it? You'll have the strength of purpose to do all that's required, at any rate. It could even mean going elsewhere and moving to new frontiers – a shift of home/office or even setting up a second establishment.

19 July: First Quarter in Libra

Once again, house and home are in the spotlight – maybe it's getting settled in a new place, as a continuation of last week's forecast. Taking care of family, parents, children, in-laws, coping with domestic responsibilities, but also, the joys and comforts of home life. Others will share in the process of decision making, including, perhaps, even your colleagues, brothers and sisters, friends.

27 July: Full Moon in Aquarius

Money and honey will be the prime factors in your life right now. Romance and love will prosper with a changed attitude of understanding and sharing things that concern you, with your loved ones. In the field of finance, you'll be looking at loans and funds, joint finance, even insurance. Travel is likely too for work rather than pleasure, and there could be delays and hold-ups; traffic dislocation and such, even while commuting short distances.

4 August: Last Quarter in Taurus

There will be passion and fire in the theme of love introduced last week. On the money scene, there will be the new players of ancestral wealth, legacy, inheritance, gains from property. Also, a fair amount of social life this quarter, good times with children, plenty of fun and games – literally, not figuratively. Overspending on entertainment or overenthusiasm in partying could lead to trouble, and I don't only mean health-wise.

11 August: New Moon in Leo

You will experience a tremendous desire to excel and shine at work or in your profession. Therefore, you put in the sheer slogging, the intense effort that will make this happen. Recognition, respect and status will be won. You'll have to devote a large measure of your time and effort to financial matters, most particularly in the realm of estate duty and problems, taxes, expenses and expense accounts, legacies and gifts, profit sharing and percentages.

18 August: First Quarter in Scorpio

You will intellectually examine and perceive emotional issues about your career, home and individual identity. You'll realize and appreciate the need for harmony in the home, as well as making it linked to your own inner self. To make all this a reality, you'll be willing, if not eager, to make that extra effort, go that extra mile. All these are a means of fulfilling your own inner urges and impulses.

26 August: Full Moon in Pisces

A somewhat esoterically exciting week. Your creative instincts and impulses bloom and grow spectacularly. A sense of beauty and aestheticism will make you look at the world around with an assessing eye trying to invest even mundane articles with beauty as well as functionality and utility. This will spill over even into the everyday activities of domestic life.

3 September: Last Quarter in Gemini

A good deal of travel, and spiralling expenses this week. Visitors, particularly from abroad, will be important, so also foreign connection. This will be particularly true on the work front. I must emphasize here – Ganesha compels me to do so – that you will need to exercise a lot of care, discretion, restraints, particularly in money matters. You will need to not only conserve your money but also to revamp present financial resources; saving for your old age or a rainy day will also be wise move.

9 September: New Moon in Virgo

You will be doing a lot of 'social' work with a difference, in terms of a pivotal role in arranging a wedding ceremony, religious service/rites, attending religious ceremonies or an interview. The last will see you displaying generosity, leadership and a true desire to serve. Future plans and objectives, political and religious disputes, and dealing with in-laws will all be highlighted. Religion and faith will be playing an important part in all your activities.

16 September: First Quarter in Sagittarius

The two things that will be vitally, even intensely, important, will be a) your work at present and b) your plans/vision for the future. The theme of social commitment to causes will be genuine and sincere. The ability to bond with others and also to work steadily and quietly behind the scenes, away from the public eye, will pay dividends.

25 September: Full Moon in Aries

A far, far better phase is now ushered in. The unsettling and troubled times of last week and earlier will fade away, despite the occasional hindrance or disappointment that you might face. Name, recognition, glory will be yours. It's time for you to work hard, of course, but the mood will be upbeat and enthusiastic. You will be quite secure in the knowledge that Ganesha says that you will go places, win plaudits and glory.

2 October: Last Quarter in Cancer

Your persona, private and public image, will be evaluated, assessed, and if found wanting, will be in for a thorough and complete overhaul – from clothes, jewels, accessories, physique, health, speech, even your mindset and total attitude to life. Diet, exercise, wardrobe – everything comes within the ambit of this makeover. You'll clean up your act, try to resolve personal issues and problems.

9 October: New Moon in Libra

As part of the theme of 2 October or perhaps an extension of it, you will turn to house, home, land, and of course, your property too for this overhaul. Parents, elderly people and in-laws, their pensions, assets, old-age benefits as well as your own, will be dealt with and thought upon. Primarily, of course, the twilight of your own life as it should be.

16 October: First Quarter in Capricorn

It's time to relax – now that you've got yourself and your home where you want them to be. Work pressures will be constant, but you will learn to live around them – take time off for parties, outings, gallivanting, shopping. Some domestic pressures too, but they'll really be a non-issue, as your present mindset will not let them escalate. Perhaps you have taken Ganesha as your role model in that respect!

24 October: Full Moon in Taurus

The focus right now, and through the coming of November, will be firmly on shared activities, pooled resources, group outings and fun as clubs, amusement parks, even dancing the night away at the disco, wining and dining in right royal style. The company you keep will be wonderfully cordial and congenial. Pleasant times all round. All this not only lets you take a breather, but truly get your second wind.

31 October: Last Quarter in Leo

The holiday mood will be over, in one sense, or perhaps you'll start finding work itself a kind of holiday, as there'll be so much fun and excitement in it. This will be in the form of capital formation, fund-raising, funds, investments – the mega-buck scene! Also, social and personal interactions, in addition to such family bonds that go back – and ahead – a whole lifetime. You're careful of the feelings of others, not wanting to hurt or antagonize anyone, treading softly in tense situations.

7 November: New Moon in Scorpio

It's a phase when it seems that, miraculously, Ganesha is making everything work out smoothly. You'll be not only successful, but happy along with it – that's rare, especially in today's world. You'll meet old friends, make new ones, socialize and be part of family activities in a pleasing, heart-warming way. Shared hopes for the future, like-minded people, comrades at work – they're all there. Finances too are favoured and there will be income from business in a steady, pleasing flow.

15 November: First quarter in Aquarius

Rise in social status and position, good times and warm, pleasant interaction with friends will be highlighted this month. You'll set your sights firmly and definitely on your plans and goals for the future and steer straight towards them. What's more, you'll find the right people to share and help in this vision of what the millennium will bring. You'll be appreciated and understood and, believe me, it's a very pleasant feeling!

23 November: Full Moon in Gemini

Please read the sentence just above. It will help you to get the right perspective on the rather high expenses you have to deal with. Thankfully, you have the money for it. New ventures may be planned or brainstormed about or even set up as well. Relationships of all kinds – friends, parents, children, loved ones – will all be specially favoured. What will not be favoured is your health – there could be posers there. Common sense dictates adequate safeguards. Just do it, orders Ganesha.

30 November: Last Quarter in Virgo

All of what I've said just above, in the previous quarter's forecast, is because of the impact of Saturn, supposedly the lame planet. He certainly causes delays, hurdles, hiccups. Travel could have snags and delays, so too could there be compromises and cancellations. Communication on an interpersonal level – in terms of interviews, settlements to be worked out, one-to-one negotiations. You have to be careful. Ganesha repeats the warning sternly.

7 December: New Moon in Sagittarius

Delays and postponements will continue, also mix-ups – in the areas of travel, interviews and important projects. In fact, you might even have to abandon a trip/journey or a project! Work pressures and demands will be high. Fears, worries, even neuroses will have to be dealt with. But there is a way out, and you see it. Obstacles to progress will be identified and removed. You do it by getting support from others, and by learning to turn your rivals/enemies into friends, comrades and well-wishers. And that is no mean feat!

15 December: First Quarter in Pisces

Your inner psyche, your intellect, avenues to peace of mind are going to be very important to you. You may undertake higher education and study, research, even travel to broaden the vistas of the mind. Good interaction with friends, the supportive and caring attitude of your mate/spouse and love will give you much pleasure and comfort. You yourself will be more caring, more sympathetic, warmer and that makes for solace and joy for yourself, as well as others.

22 December: Full Moon in Cancer

The year concludes with promise of much better things and much better times in the year 2019. The millennium's gifts to you are better health, hope for the future, enduring happiness. Social reform, spiritual growth, concern for and involvement with humanitarian causes will be important. Closer to home, it's your own home and family, even the extended family.

29 December: Last Quarter in Libra

The shift/move I spoke of could quite easily be a move up the ladder, promotions, or even taking up a home-based business. All this will be made possible by the tremendous gains in power, prestige, reputation that come your way now. Not necessarily money. It is not, and should not be, the yardstick for success. You just may, in fact, decide to take a thorough look at your capacities for moneymaking and want to try something new and different.

AQUARIUS

23 January–22 February

'Come together! Speak together!
Let your minds be in harmony,
As the Gods of old together,
Sat in harmony to worship.'

Core of Hindu religion. Also, it applies wonderfully well to our own Aquarian age. Through contacts, communication, consciousness, technology, we are now totally interconnected. It is amazing how the very old and the completely new go into each other.

- **Element:** Air

- **Ruling planet:** Uranus

- **Quality:** Fixed (= stability)

- **Qualities most needed for balance:** Warmth, feeling and emotion

- **Day:** Saturday.

- **Gemstone:** Black pearl, obsidian, opal, sapphire, aquamarine.

- **Colours:** Aquamarine, turquoise and electric blue, grey, ultramarine

- **Scents:** Azalea, gardenia

- **Metals:** Uranium and aluminium

- **Countries:** Russia, Sweden, Ethiopia and Poland

- **Number:** Four, one and seven

Special Message from Bejan and Nastur: Ganesha says, yours is the perfect example of yin and yang. The balance of two opposite forces. Saturn in your twelfth house makes you introspective and spiritual. Jupiter in your tenth house makes you extrovert and completely practical. Your speciality is a broad intellectual vision of humanity. You are an original thinker. Original thinkers are often slightly crazy. The world needs more people like you. That's for sure.

JUPITER

Jupiter will be in your lucky and exceptionally favourable tenth angle from 10 October 2017 to 8 November 2018. 'To will is to select a goal, determine a course of action that will bring one to that goal, and the hold to that action till the goal is reached. The key is action.' – Michael Hanson. How come Ganesha has focalized on this for you?

Jupiter will be at the meridian, the zenith, in your solar-scope, with these results:

a) Prestige, power, position, perks, pelf – the five Ps will be yours.

b) Like Sania Mirza and Saina Nehwal, you too will be an outright winner in the to-and-fro badminton of life, the greatest game of all, because life is the final and most dramatic of all contests!

c) Responsibility in irreversible, monumental proportions will be thrust upon you, but that will give you the authority and ability to handle pressure, and that's ultimately important.

d) Prestige does a huge pole vault; parents figure in your scheme of things, inheritance and possession will show up on the Internet of your individual life. You learn to play splendidly with all kinds of new-fangled gadgets, and the various media of communication.

e) The health of parents, elders and in-laws could, however, cause concern; the same goes for boss and superiors.

f) Your proficiency, performance will be at an all-time high and this should give you the necessary confidence to achieve your targets/goals. In practical terms this is what astrology is all about – giving confidence!

g) Honours, awards, rewards sum it all up nicely.

The tenth house also refers to popularity, authority, responsibility – the three personality factors which decide our destiny.

SATURN

By Western astrology, Saturn will be in your twelfth angle from 21 December 2017 to 22 March 2020. Saturn stands for limitations and determinations. The twelfth angle represents:

a) Heavy expenses on account of relatives, poor health, poor losses;

b) Hospitalization, charities, social work, welfare activities;

c) Hidden secrets and clandestine activities;

d) Foreign collaboration and ties;

e) Open and envious, as well as secret enemies and conspiracies;

f) A home away from home is also a distinct possibility, as with the Jupiter placing. In life and in astrology there are no certainties, though. Property matters are also foretold;

g) All confidential and personal affairs will be strongly focalized. Sometimes you may suffer a setback in reputation and prestige;

h) Try to be less critical and more tolerant in your behaviour and attitude. Believe me, it will help.

i) Take expert advice and guidance where necessary and don't simmer and suffocate yourself.

Luckily in 2018, Jupiter and Saturn will be in a fine and benefic formation. It will help you in two ways: a) property matters, b) reduction in losses than they would, otherwise be. But there is a danger of robbery, loss or misplacing of documents, valuables and possessions.

URANUS

On and after 4 March 2019, Uranus moves outside your third angle. This is the last year where Uranus remains in your third angle of invention, rebellion, disruption and also innovation. Without conflict, there is no drama and many times no creativity. This is the great secret. I am revealing it to you now because I am eighty-six years old and writing it on 22 December 2016. Good Luck to you, now and always, dear Aquarians.

NEPTUNE

Neptune helps you in terms of delicious food, imaginative speech and sudden rise in income, may be a promotion. My only request is, do not indulge yourself beyond limits. A little moderation helps.

PLUTO

Pluto stays with Saturn in your twelfth angle, making you dynamic in your compassion, service to others and health to others. You will work like a warhorse to aid others. Obviously, this will do you a lot of good. Good clear impulses and waves will emanate from you around the whole world.

MONTHLY ROUND-UPS

January: Work and projects could tell on your health unless you learn to relax; **February**: Love/hate, attachments/separations, journey/home away from home, marriage/divorce; **March**: Funds for work/home, trusts, buying/selling/investing/capital formation; **April**: Journeys, publicity, exultation, collaborations, a grand reaching out to people and places; **May**: 'Work is worship' could well be your motto. For good measure, add duty and beauty; **June**: Love, life, laughter, and the law of chances operates in your favour; so if you feel like it, take a few chances; **July**: Despite expenses and interferences, property matters and family conditions do give some satisfaction; buying/selling/journeying are emphasized;

August: Go all out for the kill, and emerge victorious in whatever you do; **September**: Finances and funds will be augmented; **October**: Contacts, contracts, socializing, friendship, good news and you; **November**: Home, house, family, parents, property, renovation/decoration, buying/selling/leasing/shopping; **December**: Plenty of fun and frolic, children and creativity fulfil you. A great ending to a busy beginning, concludes Ganesha.

HAPPINESS QUOTA: 80 per cent

WEEKLY REVIEW (BY PHASES OF THE MOON)

2 January: Full Moon in Cancer

Ganesha says if I were asked to sum up in one word what you'll be doing in this first quarter of the millennium, the word I'd use is *reach*. Within its reach will be the usual ones of people and places – communications and travel, in other words. I don't need to explain further, I'm sure. Living up to your sign, you will also reach out to help the physically and mentally challenged.

8 January: Last Quarter in Libra

Socializing, cementing friendships, joining clubs, social organizations improving your social standing are all there for you. A challenging situation could develop regarding work responsibilities, but you'll meet the demands it makes on you with style and aplomb. The most pleasing, in fact heart-warming, part of it all will be the love you share, in either an old or a new relationship around this time.

17 January: New Moon in Capricorn

The trend of questioning and analysing of the first quarter of the year takes a detour to include finances. Loans and funds, employment and perks, old and new projects will be viewed in this light. The reason could even be a change of job/work/ profession. You may even have to tighten the purse strings – both personal and for business, at least temporarily. Don't feel too burdened by the responsibilities you're shouldering.

24 January: First Quarter in Taurus

Follow the voice within you, call it conscience, superego, what you will. The advice will be hard work, knowing what you need to do to fulfil your desire for excellence. You just might want to win out over adversaries, bag that project or contract, gain a promotion/position. Power struggles will find you striving hard. We all do it at times, even I – though I'd rather be an astrologer than anything else.

31 January: Full Moon in Leo

There will be revolutionary changes in both your outlook and environment, investing everything you do with the aura of success. You'll be full of feelings of self-worth, confidence – in yourself and in the future. There will be noticeable gains in both personal acquisitions, belongings, as well as money in the bank or in your wallet. All in all, you acquire a bright new image – both externally and within yourself.

7 February: Last Quarter in Scorpio

You'll be ready to grasp financial opportunities, to devote extra time to money matters, perhaps even meeting the people who can create the opportunities you're looking for. But the focus of your attention will be house, home, property. Either acquiring or renovation, decoration, extension, repairs will be what you'll be doing primarily. Perhaps it's this focus that will trigger your financial activities or vice versa.

15 February: New Moon in Aquarius

Once again, your income-generating ability, the capacity to earn so that you can keep pace with life in the new millennium will be emphasized. You will focus, therefore, on your career and business activities. There will be distractions in the shape of family responsibilities and commitments, perhaps even legal issues, which will have to be dealt with and cannot be delegated.

23 February: First Quarter in Gemini

Your personality will shine through, as your sphere of interests and achievements expands. The maximum gain will be spectacular success at socializing, friendship, receiving and giving love. You'll be fiercely independent, full of self-confidence and zest, so much so that you could even become a victim of mental fatigue.

2 March: Full Moon in Virgo

Jupiter bestows gains, property, finance, friendship, fraternity, in addition to ever-increasing self-knowledge. But right now, there is security from money in the bank, which influences the joys from family life, hospitality, visitors and guests, social interaction. It's a good phase that will continue, off and on, right into June. Food, family, finances – the three Fs – are most definitely emphasized.

9 March: Last Quarter in Sagittarius

A spectacular boost in vision, optimism, the will to make things happen, mental growth and expansion – an impressive list indeed! There will be friendly activity to support all this. Hobbies and sports, loving times with children, even success at speculation. Avenues like research, inventions, information technology, space travel, astrology and also tantra and mantra will draw you, and could even be work-related.

17 March: New Moon in Pisces

You now come down to earth in a different, practical way. The nitty-gritty of finances and domestic responsibilities will have you a) dealing with buying/selling, fund-raising, investments; b) acquiring gadgets, luxuries, lifestyle enhancers, objets d'art for the home; c) shopping for new clothes, jewels, accessories, making over your wardrobe and your image.

24 March: First Quarter in Cancer

I promise you, it'll be one of the most hectic, frenzied weeks you've experienced for a long time. Finances and creative abilities may be found short, so you'll go all out, experimenting, innovating, implementing new ideas. These new ideas may easily extend into a love affair, romance and passion. There can be liaisons (of the kind mentioned just above) or for business and also some frantic, secret activities, some kind of wheeling-dealing, bargaining and manoeuvring.

31 March: Full Moon in Libra

Once again, I can use a single word to sum up the trend for the month: relationships. These will range from casual to personal to professional to influential. Bonds and connections in all possible varieties will be the keynote. Therefore, it goes without saying that any kind of negativism or lack of cooperation on your part could prove mighty dangerous.

8 April: Last Quarter in Capricorn

Despite contrary pulls, you show vision, optimism, grace under pressure and of course, hard unrelenting work. It will all start paying off now. Pending matters will be solved and resolved, new ventures/projects will get the 'go ahead' sign. Travel too is strongly indicated, though actually speaking, it could have happened last week as well. Right now, it's all the Ps – from pets to pelf, power, position, prestige, promotion that are the strong, clear astrological indications.

16 April: New Moon in Aries

Your personal values, lifestyle, inner foundations will see a shift, a revision. The result will, perhaps most importantly, be joy in your relations with parents, family and, most particularly, children. In the house of earnings and income, there will be a loan/endowment/grant, and the definite possibility of entering into some new collaboration, tie-up or partnership. That comes within the scope of the values and lifestyle that I spoke of at the very beginning of this forecast.

22 April: First Quarter in Leo

The crying need for generating a larger income will possess you. You'll realize that it's necessary if you want to implement the new values, plans/expectations that we spoke of in the last quarter. The fields for useful work could cover worthy causes like service to the needy, social welfare, philanthropy, secret charity, even larger global concerns. You'll do it not for publicity and glory as some people do, but out of genuine concern for the world, and yourself as a part of it.

30 April: Full Moon in Scorpio

Domestic harmony, family relationships, household matters will be all your main concerns. Also, matter related to property and house – and their renovation, improvement, beautification. Older relatives and in-laws will be in the picture too this week and through the period. All these are monthly trends too, please remember. There will be pleasure, creativity and much personal liberty despite the concerns I just mentioned, but also, unfortunately, some posers regarding your health.

8 May: Last Quarter in Aquarius

Communications, contacts, leading to contracts. I have to fall back on one of my oft-used phrases since it sums up what relationships will now expand to mean. New acquaintances, new places can both prove to be profitable in the future. Lifetime bonds and ties are favoured. That's if you play your cards well – there is the danger or discarding an ace in terms of losing the affection of someone you love. However, people and places are important.

15 May: New Moon in Taurus

Aquarians are great ones for hard work, which they tackle cheerfully and quite enjoy – unlike yours truly! There will be the due rewards and fallouts for you. I forgot to mention that an unfavourable Sun–Saturn conjunction took place. All this busy planetary activity bestows on you – publicity, perks, promotions, pleasure, pelf – wonderful Ps! Ganesha shares your joy!

22 May: First Quarter in Virgo

Now comes better health, the capacity for even harder work, better relations with loved ones and children. And doesn't Aquarians, the ultimate carer and provider, just love it? There's much more romance, entertainment, joie de vivre, so that you lighten up a lot. If you think that's all – there's the final pièce de résistance – absolutely outstanding charisma and creativity, greater personal liberty.

29 May: Full Moon in Sagittarius

The last three words above could, truly speaking, sum up the trend for June; along with everything being fine and dandy; you're sailing on a sea as smooth as glass! Great rapport with young people, even your own children, much zest and enjoyment, recreation, old and new hobbies, sports, games, leisure pursuits. You not only have the time and inclination but the funds to enjoy it all! New, exciting possibilities open up a vista of exceptional achievement.

6 June: Last Quarter in Pisces

There will be a total, if not drastic turnabout, a volte-face as they say in French, about your priorities in life. It's finances, money, big-time career advancement and financial success! You will think of ways and means to increase your income, generate fresh sources of earning. The astrological reason is the continued placing of Jupiter in May. The other practical, material reason is that you need to spend on renovation, improvement, enhancement of your office/

workplace/business premises or necessities related to the expansion of these.

13 June: New Moon in Gemini

There is a brilliance about you that is manifested in several ways: a) brilliantly successful relationships at work with colleagues, co-workers, superiors who will be important for you; b) performing brilliantly at conferences, meetings and in partnerships, teamwork; c) the races, the casino. Wherever you care to chance your arm in this moon quarter, you're bound to strike it rich. And it's not just money I'm referring to. Neither is Ganesha.

20 June: First Quarter in Virgo

If you were feeling your oats last week, now you're ready to accept the bit, the bridle and saddle meekly. Domestic matters and your family will totally occupy your attention, and also property, legal matters, finances – all in the context of the home and family. You will, however, exhibit the gentle and caring side of your nature on a larger scale too – in your concern for the poor, the sick, the infirm and the needy, even the universe and the ecology, the environment.

28 June: Full Moon in Capricorn

It's people, people and different people that will be the focus this quarter with happy outcomes from this interfacing exercise. Domestic and family issues will definitely improve, especially your relationship with your spouse/partner. You'll have to give of yourself to children, dependents, servants, even pets – in terms of time, looking after, nurturing or even playing nursemaid/protector.

6 July: Last Quarter in Aries

There will be much gain from what kept you busy last week. Firstly, there is much happiness in personal relationships now. You'll set a fine, spanking pace at work. In the field of academics, higher study, new disciplines and avenues of learning, you'll really dazzle and shine. Even if it's discoveries, a new software package or 'just' the Net you're into. Health will need to be guarded, or more correctly, adequate rest and avoidance of strain are what are required.

13 July: New Moon in Cancer

Success in money matters is assured this week, after Moon and Sun formed a trine or beneficial placing on the eleventh. This was a powerful one – incidentally, that's my birthday. I'm not claiming any credit – just mentioning it in passing! Long-cherished hopes and dreams may be realized, even though expenses will be painfully high. I can assure you it'll be worth it. Remember that dreadful saying we Indians have, 'no pain, no gain'. Ugly expression, but true!

19 July: First Quarter in Libra

There will be much travel and also great fanfare attached to your activities, as you ride the crest of a wave in terms of success. No more money worries, that's for sure. Be careful not to run up debts, or make bad investments. Go over fresh contracts, deeds, documents with a fine-toothed comb, or there could be goof-ups and blunders in profit sharing that will cost you dearly.

27 July: Full Moon in Aquarius

New beginnings, travel and trips and journeys, and also partnerships are highlighted. An exciting start to a new venture/project could occur. Most importantly, perhaps the partnership I mentioned could be the best one of all – love and marriage. There is bound to be a lot of love in marriage, or even otherwise. Perhaps you'll fall in love for the first time – what could possibly be more exciting? Delayed projects too will get rejuvenated, just like the way love makes you feel.

4 August: Last Quarter in Taurus

It's not just love and relationships that you'll be a whizz at now, but the wheeling-dealing, demanding yet thrilling game of big-time business. Power will be your middle name at business meetings, conferences, presentations. In fact it's most likely that you'll be the mover and shaker, the initiator, for new projects/ventures/undertakings/launches. The terrestrial reason: you'll have funds flowing in for business, and as they say, the man who pays the piper calls the tune!

11 August: New Moon in Leo

Confidence, charisma, charm ooze out of you. There will be no doubt in your mind, and also in the minds of those around you, who the victor is in the battleground of life right now. And to the victor, the spoils of war. Success, meeting of targets/objectives, the money in the bank, peace and harmony in the home, love in your heart and in that of your mate/partner/spouse/lover. What largesse from Ganesha!

18 August: First Quarter in Scorpio

After splendid activity and equally splendid success, your thoughts wend their way homeward, as warriors did after victorious battles. See, I've maintained the analogy. You'll be on a spending spree that's the Big Daddy of all sprees. Extending and improving your wardrobe, your assets, property, home, jewels, family luxuries, the latest in cars, gadgets, objets d'art. You name it, you buy it. If you're successful, you've got to show it – that is the modern school of thought. And that's what you're doing right now, in the millennium.

26 August: Full Moon in Pisces

Money and moving, to sum up the trend for the coming month. Money will relate to loans, funds, capital, inheritance, legacies, property. Moving will be: a) emotional development of new ties or attitudes to loved ones, a touch of romance, intense passion; b) moving house, or from city, place, country to a new one. This last could be for both the reasons, or either love or money, the two prime motivators of the millennium, as from time immemorial.

3 September: Last Quarter in Gemini

This will be a fine week for you. You are not afraid of hard work, Aquarians, and are known to relish it, in fact. Sometimes you can be a bit too serious, but certainly not this week, where your attitude to rest, relaxation, recreation is concerned. Amusements, partying, socializing – generally enjoying yourself. It's a good time you're having, doing all this and more. What will make it truly special is the way you interact with people of all kinds, ages, predispositions. It's rare and beautiful to behold.

9 September: New Moon in Virgo

There has been a beautiful trine between Venus and Jupiter on eighth. Less this week and much more in the week to follow, the effect will be felt in terms of power and money. For you, Aquarians, it is time to deal with a) finances of all kinds; b) business transactions and; c) legal matters. In this last item on my list for you, the astrological advice from Ganesha would be to negotiate, compromise, even go in for an out-of-court settlement rather than get drawn into a prolonged legal battle.

16 September: First Quarter in Sagittarius

The effect of the trine is to be seen now in all its glory. There's nothing you're not doing right now. Escapades, adventures, risky deals being pulled off, intense love affairs, passionate interludes, spiritual pursuits, tantra and mantra – most specially, and also travel. You will certainly be travelling between now and the end of this year, also important are communications of all kinds. If I said 'money and moving' three weeks ago, now I'd say it's movement and messages.

25 September: Full Moon in Aries

What will firm up will the be trend of travel, trips and movement. Attendance in meetings, conferences, conventions, interviews and presentations will happen – all this with a view to future plans and objectives, your place in the world, and millennium-wise, in the universe. Remember, this is a monthly trend which has long-term and long-range implications. You'll learn to relate better to people, perhaps master the principles of art of living, investigate the New Age values, jettison 'wrong' values and career aims.

2 October: Last Quarter in Cancer

Esoteric activities and concerns, secret deals, arcane pursuits will be one side of the picture. The other – care and help for the sick, infirm, mentally challenged and the deprived, sometimes referred to as the flotsam and jetsam of society.

Travel and/or travel plans will be definite, perhaps to welfare centres, homes for the aged, hospices and places of healing. It is in this that most Aquarians really come into their own. And this week, at least, you will be no exception.

9 October: New Moon in Libra

Your performance and commitment to the world of intellectual and academic activities will be mind-blowing. Self-improvement and self and God realization will compel you. In this search for the link between the atman and Brahma will not only make you introspect, meditate but also take up courses of study, new skills, research, even learn a new technical trade/degree. This last to fulfil your responsibilities in the material world.

16 October: First Quarter in Capricorn

Monetary fallouts in terms of job benefits may be seen. Also, the handling of funds, capital, assets and loans for future gain. There will be total commitment to and absorption in your work sphere, and yet you'll be pursuing equally high objectives in terms of duties and ties as a parent, or to your parents. Also, elderly relatives, in-laws, and improvement of your surroundings, your home. All this adds up to a feeling of great joy and warmth, comfort and security.

24 October: Full Moon in Taurus

All kinds of avenues and opportunities for gain, improvement of job prospects or advancement in life now open up. The sextile of Venus and Neptune on 22 October bestows gains in both material and spiritual earnings. You'll move ahead full of zest, dedication, power, wishing to make others as well as yourself recognize your true worth. Achievement and recognition beckon you, in the guise of Ganesha.

31 October: Last Quarter in Leo

In this quarter of your own birth sign, there is greater power, strength of purpose, energy, vitality, zest – you name it! Professional or business success, along with credit, popularity, power and authority. And you handle it well. Peace and harmony in the home are vitally important for you and you will strive to maintain them at all costs, abandoning pride and ego.

7 November: New Moon in Scorpio

You will find this week and the next week vital, pivotal, totally so, for consolidating, firming up the gains you've made so far. It's not necessary to look at new beginnings but rather to consolidate your position like our troops digging in, bunker by bunker, on the Kargil front, never letting go. Family ties and bonds will be renewed and rejuvenated. Also, your home, which could come in for a major facelift. But, you'll now not so much be buying new things as redoing, refurbishing, refurnishing.

15 November: First Quarter in Aquarius

Friends and acquaintances will now come within the ambit of this phase and need for drawing close, and your loved ones and family too. It's one large, magical circle of affection and warmth. A good way to be, comments Ganesha, that champion at caring and family. Romance, engagements, wedding bells too are to be made out in the atmosphere, or the not too distant future – our own, or of someone close.

23 November: Full Moon in Gemini

A slightly different trend for the month – I'd call it a detour or deviation which meets up with the same path you've treaded over the last three or four weeks. Socializing, group activities, meetings, outings, entertaining, the giving and taking of hospitality. You'll have weighed up and decided who your true friends are, and what your own true values are, as well. A long-nurtured ambition, wish, dream can finally be realized too.

30 November: Last Quarter in Virgo

You are firm and determined in your resolve, and work hard and long to achieve what you want out of life. What you'll get this week will be money by the fistful; the Midas touch is yours. But there's appreciation both professionally and at home along with popularity, admiration and approval. As a special gift, there may be a welcome addition to, or new birth in, the family. You will feel doubly blessed by Ganesha.

7 December: New Moon in Sagittarius

Once again, your popularity, credit, authority, social standing register a further rise on the graph, like the Sensex zooming. Most importantly perhaps, you feel wonderful, not just good, about yourself. Ganesha compels me to warn you against getting carried away by the euphoria generated over the last two months. The millennium could bring you down with a thud, unless you fuse and balance work and recreation, home and business.

15 December: First Quarter in Pisces

There'll be a kind of single-point programme or agenda in your life in this quarter, the penultimate one of the year 2018, and that will be the front of finances and money matters. Nothing else will be as important this week. Or should we say, nothing else requires your attention. Capital raising, funds, lending, borrowing, buying and selling. Almost all financial activities will be emphatically demanding. Perhaps as a corollary, there could be a house/office move.

22 December: Full Moon in Cancer

The year 2018 now ends in the same quarter on which it started. Socializing, relationships with friends, networking, cementing bonds and relationships will be the major focus not just this week, but as the overall pattern for your life, in the new millennium. I wonder if I need to remind you that the millennium means a thousand years – that's certainly how long it will seem that your love will last. It's truly heart-warming this quarter, at any rate.

29 December: Last Quarter in Libra

It's a good time to take that long-deferred holiday, visit adventure parks, take up a sport, invent a new game, or practise your strokes in cricket/golf or whatever. If not, follow the amusements that draw you, even if it's going to the casino in Las Vegas or Monte Carlo. The luck of the draw and the fall of the dice favour you, even if it's just making an investment in the stock market. You learn to compromise on major differences with partners, be they at business or in life!

PISCES

23 February–20 March

Ganesha says biopharmaceuticals will rule and ride the chemical world in 2018. Pisces is an ideal medium for it. Ganesha says it is time to be quick and curious, time to use the immense power of medicinal plants, time to know the four *mahavakya*s, the essence of the Upanishads. Each mahavakya represents a Veda, namely Rig Veda, Sama Veda, Yajur Veda and Atharva Veda. The essence: *Aham brahmasmi*. Yes, Pisces are very spiritual and therefore I have drawn your attention to it.

- **Element:** Water

- **Ruling planet:** Neptune

- **Quality:** Mutability (= flexibility)

- **Qualities most needed for balance:** Structure and the ability to handle form

- **Strongest virtues:** Psychic power, sensitivity, self-sacrifice, altruism

- **Day:** Thursday

- **Scent:** Lotus

- **Symbolic interpretation:** Two fishes tied to one another in opposite directions, signifying hidden depths, shifting emotional currents – the symbol representing two fishes tied together, also a picture of the human feet (the part of the anatomy that Pisces rules)

- **Hazards:** Pisceans can be unpredictable, vacillating and indecisive; unbalanced, and prone to addictions

- **Gemstone:** Amethyst

- **Metals:** Germanium and strontium, tin, white diamond

- **Colours:** Mauve, purple, violet, sea green, silver

- **Numbers:** Seven, two and six

- **Flowers:** White poppy, iris, orchid, water lily, angelica, violet, jonquil

- **Trees:** Weeping willow, all trees growing by water, fig

- **Foods:** Foods with a high water content, such as cucumber, watermelon, lettuce, and the gourd family

Special Message from Bejan and Nastur: Ganesha says my devotee Bejan Daruwalla has observed that Pisces is the last sign. Therefore, something or other of all the other eleven signs percolates into Pisces. Pisces can be indecisive, very evolved, emotional, imaginative, spiritual, but it drinks; and drunks should be avoided. Einstein, the greatest scientist of the twentieth century, was a Piscean. Also, they are the escape artist of the zodiac. They can be very lonely in a crowd. Best example is the Piscean Jayalalithaa.

JUPITER

Jupiter will be in your ninth angle from 21 December 2017

to 22 March 2020. Ganesha says, pushing the envelope is a typical American expression. For example, a test pilot tests the jet to its extreme capacity and power. Therefore, the test pilot is pushing the envelope. Both the major planets, Jupiter and Saturn, huff and puff for you. First, let us take Jupiter the planet of progress, expansion and good luck which will be in your ninth angle this year.

Napoleon the great believed in recruiting 'lucky soldiers' for his famous 'Old Guard'. Nearer home, Bill Gates, the richest man in the world, said, 'Success is a mixture of work, belief in what you are doing, and a bit of luck.' In cricket a catch may make all the difference between losing and winning.

Here is the special advice for you Pisceans, you must learn to do well from group activities, be part of the team in large organizations, fit in the social circles.

SATURN

By Western astrology, Saturn will be in your eleventh angle from 21 December 2017 to 22 March 2020. Let us now talk about the grandmaster of the planets, namely Saturn.

Saturn, stern taskmaster and consolidator extraordinary, has been crawling away (Saturn is a slow-moving planet) in your eleventh angle, resulting in:

a) Mood, elevation, depression, i.e., swings, ceremony, evolution of the spirit;

b) Research and higher learning, real wisdom, long-distance journeys and connections;

c) Parents, elders, in-laws will figure very prominently in your scheme of things, and there is some danger to their health and well-being; therefore, a medical check-up will be a good idea. Do remember, it is merely a suggestion;

d) Future plans and even mighty campaigns will be planned and that's the heart of the matter.

Saturn will continue in your eleventh angle. Saturn will consolidate your wishes. Paradoxically, Saturn will also cause delays. But Saturn, though slow-moving, is sure-footed. Therefore, have faith, and good things are bound to happen. In the last two years, you must have ended relationships as well as started ties and alliances. The focus is strong and clear, must have been on friendships and gains in the last two years. Saturn can bestow a long-lasting friendship. Saturn can give you ideals, hopes and wishes. You may, actually I am sure you do, have a few outside friends who are solid, stable, secure. They will stand by you. If you have any difficulty in dealing with people in a very open and direct manner, do not blame yourself overmuch. This placing of Saturn is directly responsible for it.

Saturn will be in your eleventh angle, which signifies:

a) gains of all types, incomes, acquisition;

b) fulfilment of desires, nature of earning, rewards, arrival;

c) recognition, favours from the boss, special status, proficiency, learning, ancestral property, fondness for precious stones;

d) lost wealth, pursuit of pious and religious deeds, profits and returns;

e) the elder brother, paternal uncle, longevity of the mother, material enjoyments.

All the above events will evidently not happen. The crux or real problem is that Pisceans will have mixed results. Why? Saturn is the planet of limitation and sorrow. Pisces is the sign of expansion and power. These planetary placing are by Western astrology only. Saturn in Pisces is uncomfortable and unhappy. A few of your desires and goals will be realized. But a few will flop and fail. Once you know this you will be prepared for any eventuality. The result will be less hurt, less disappointment, less frustration. This is what astrology is all about. It is about making you happier at times, and other times, guiding you to be less unhappy. in other words, it is about guiding you to the path of life. No discipline is perfect therefore astrology is not perfect either.

Here is special advice for you Pisceans. You must learn to do well in group activities, be part of the team in large organizations, fit in the social circles and whirligig. Let me put it in a different way. Your secret of success will be in your ability to adjust and accommodate. If you do so, your gains and joy, your profit and your pleasure, will all be doubled. Otherwise expenses and losses are all likely. Now the choice is yours. The stars only impel, but they do not compel. Children and grandchildren, plans and projects, romance and speculation, promotion and perks, prestige and power – all come under the ambit and influence of Saturn in your eleventh angle.

Jupiter and Saturn will be in lucky formation, helping you to reach your goals, have your heart's desire, reach out to people and places. In one word, fulfilment, to some extent. Ganesha willing, it is possible. This is good news for you.

Neptune and Jupiter are your main planets, but for you Mercury also plays an important part. From 9 January to

13 February Mercury helps you in all group activities and social connection. The period from 5 to 21 March is certainly ideal for contacts, communication, love, travel, pilgrimage and group activities; that from 13 to 29 June highlights the domestic scene and property and parental matters; from 30 June to 13 July, it is fun time, music time. The period from 31 July to 6 October is for romance, relationships and finance; 25 October to 12 November, for journeys, celebrations, festive occasions. Finally, 3 to 31 December once again highly favours social functions and group activities.

URANUS

Till 4 March 2019 Uranus could play merry hell in your angle of finance and family. But nothing in life is perfect and Ganesha says you have to take the rough with the smooth in real life. All in all, a thwacking good year.

NEPTUNE

Neptune, your major planet in your own sign, helps you in all creative pursuits. Aamir Khan, the Piscean, and all others will prove their worth, show their mettle and win awards and rewards. In short creation at white heat.

PLUTO

Pluto gives a big shout to all your activities connecting with the public at large. Politicians, artists, top executives, spiritual leaders will outshine everybody else.

MONTHLY ROUND-UPS

January: Open Sesame to fame, fortune, children, romance, hobbies, creativity; **February:** Health, work, colleagues, irritations over pets, projects and important trifles; **March:** Collaborations, partnerships at all levels, journeys with a stopover, reaching out to people, places; **April:** Joint finances, insurance, loans, public trusts, low vitality, sex and love in a strange mix; **May:** The luck of the draw, knowledge, evolution, wisdom, ancestors and rites, genuine spirituality, long-distance connections, pilgrimages; **June:** A high-powered month for work and play, prestige and promotion, parents and in-laws, boss and life mate; **July:** A golden harvest for the trouble taken and the seeds planted, and that says it all; **August:** Expenses, work, contacts, secret work, affairs of the heart, illumination of the soul, though there could be inflammation of your (foot) sole; **September:** Wishes granted, rewards, wish-fulfilment is possible. You will feel wonderful and strong, ready to take on anything and anybody; **October:** Finance, food, family, and that does not mean entertainment, amusement, doing the social rounds; **November:** Gains, friends, children, creativity, group activity, joy and delight in life; **December:** House, home, parents, in-laws, a home away from home, travel, get-togethers and separations.

HAPPINESS QUOTA: 87 per cent

WEEKLY REVIEW (BY PHASES OF THE MOON)

2 January: Full Moon in Cancer

The trend for the millennium, the new year, the month is initiated right now. The influence of the trine formed by Sun and Saturn makes itself felt right away. You are quite justified in being convinced that you'll go places in life. A positive mindset, attitude, approach to life and living will make it happen in a hurry. You have been quite an achiever in the past, and plan to carry on the good work. Therefore, I would say that the mood is one of looking firmly ahead at the future, forgetting the mistakes of the past but not forgetting what they've taught you.

8 January: Last Quarter in Libra

The four Fs of finance, food, family and fun will cover your activities this quarter. There's hospitality, wining and dining, entertaining galore. Good money and enhanced prestige and social status help with the good times. Also, a raise/ promotion makes it even more wonderful. The workplace will also draw you to give of your best, so that you feel all this is truly deserved.

17 January: New Moon in Capricorn

Shifting and changing things around, general reorganization – both for your home and for your own life, trying to make greater harmony, giving yourself fresh priorities. There will be the determined chase and wooing of a special someone, a loved one, who may perhaps be the motivating force behind all this. With your gentle Piscean charm, I can foresee that you'll be successful. My good wishes and congratulations on your conquest!

24 January: First Quarter in Taurus

Once again, shifts and changes are the primary factors, which you will be eager to accept and implement most happily. Right now, it's money matters that will occupy your mind – mobilizing cash, assets, ensuring a cash flow for your projects and plans. In addition to these earthly pursuits, there is also the other-worldly pursuit of spiritualism, study of occult phenomena, even questions of rebirth and reincarnation.

31 January: Full Moon in Leo

The full moon brings repose, quietness, calmness of mind and demeanour. Pisces is a sign that needs this from time to time. Right now there is for you, under the influence of Moon forming a trine with Jupiter, equal measures of both introversion and extroversion. Whatever else you do, some secret and secretive meetings, activities, perhaps, even a love affair are likely. Journeys too in the same vein. You will actually withdraw from extra complications and involvements.

7 February: Last Quarter in Scorpio

The more ways I spoke of, just two weeks ago, will be there this week too – emotional, mental, physical, financial. Money will be spectacularly easy to handle. You will experience the pride of ownership and possession in not just your assets but, more importantly, in your own self. If this tendency is kept within limits, it's fair enough, but this proprietary attitude can easily become an ego hassle with people.

15 February: New Moon in Aquarius

Your workplace, work, vocation, avocation – all these are spotlighted. You will experience a tremendous boost in self-confidence, strength of purpose, morale. Saturn – the dark planet, often misunderstood – makes for hard work, and Mercury speeds up, energizes almost all aspects of life – personal relationships, money, travel, and most particularly, career and spiritualism. It seems to be an all-inclusive list, doesn't it?

23 February: First Quarter in Gemini

The total nature of your work, and its influence and

ramifications vis-à-vis your life will undergo a sea change. You will see the successful completion of pending work, ventures, assignment, and a wonderful start to new projects. Money will be so easy as to be unbelievable and you will maintain a dazzling headstart at work, in the face of rivals, competitors, even colleagues and subordinates. There is no stopping you, says Ganesha.

2 March: Full Moon in Virgo

The full moon makes you so concerned about your image, turnout, personality, physical appearance as to seem almost obsessed by it. You will be equally concerned about, and work towards, creating/improving the image of the organization you are a part of, the superiors you represent. There is no doubt that appreciation and praise will be heaped upon you. In this fine week that Ganesha has granted you, he advises humility, learning to take a back seat, retire into the background.

9 March: Last Quarter in Sagittarius

After your brilliant performance and hard work over the last two weeks, your thoughts turn homewards – or to a pied-à-terre, a home away from home, perhaps. It's older people, parents and in-laws, relatives – the aged, in general, that you will care for, especially so, with much gentleness and concern. Pisceans are great with very old and the very young! And they are willing to put in patient effort to make things easier for them.

17 March: New Moon in Pisces

You'll be back to work with a vengeance. This is a rare phenomenon, as Pisces and Gemini, to some extent, are signs where the natives are not some of the workers of the world. You try now to make optimum use of opportunities and offers that interest you, and come your way now. Also, of your time with your family. So, it's both home and office/workplace that you are caught between and this makes for a lot of exertion and stress.

24 March: First Quarter in Cancer

Perhaps the relaxation I prescribed is being taken seriously! Whatever, it's time for laughter, fun, partying, dancing and making merry. It's time for you to have people – congenial and caring – around you, with perhaps the special person too, the one who lights up your life. Love is a strong indication around this time.

31 March: Full Moon in Libra

High adventure this month, most particularly, in the world of finance and money. You will not, however, play an entirely swashbuckling role. You'll have to sort out domestic tangles and family squabbles, and make deals at work. Business transactions and finances also find you playing the role of peacemaker, negotiator. You bring your considerable talents for tact and diplomacy into play for both home and money matters, treading carefully, trying to keep everyone contented and satisfied.

8 April: Last Quarter in Capricorn

There is now joy for you from several likely quarters, perhaps as a reward from Ganesha for our own efforts last week, to give joy to others: a) happy interaction with children keeps you delighted; b) much amusement, entertainment, partying, social interaction with people you love meeting; c) pursuit of hobbies, sports, leisure activities for pleasure; d) of course, the best of all, love from the special person who means everything to you. You may even be meeting that person around this time!

16 April: New Moon in Aries

There's so much activity in your life that you may feel it's a manic phase. Lots of movement to and fro, especially on the work front, in terms of deals, mergers, risk taking, the negotiating of loans and funds. Plenty of passion, sex, high romance, in fact, high drama in matters of the heart. You're in a mood to take risks, gamble with your money, your heart, your future. Since Ganesha is smiling at you, you may just pull it off. I forgot to mention that both last week and this one are important for both spills and thrills in finance, playing the market, speculation.

22 April: First Quarter in Leo

Work will get done smoothly, dexterously, comfortably, for you. The reason is not so much your own efficiency as your immense skill in handling people. You're good to them, and they are spectacularly good to you! This will be most specially true for friends, lovers, mate/partner/spouse, childhood loves. All your needs will be met, to some degree or other. It's your own interaction that's making it happen.

30 April: Full Moon in Scorpio

The marvellous phase of the last two weeks seems to firm up – in fact gets better all the time. And the truly wonderful part is that this is the trend for the month. This period is really likely to blossom for Pisceans. You'll have the best of both worlds, home and office, family and profession, love and money, beauty and utility. You will truly enjoy even the most mundane of chores and tasks. Your children truly have a ball with you right now. Money will flow freely but with true Piscean carelessness, you may just tend to let it fly away altogether.

8 May: Last Quarter in Aquarius

Basically, you are in for a busy period. As I frequently like to remind my readers, Saturn brings hard work. Pisceans do not really relish having to work hard, though they do it well enough and willingly enough. Right now, it will be contacts, connections in influential and/or government circles, starting up projects and collaborations that will keep you fully occupied. Rest and respite come to you from joy and pleasant moments with pets, children, dependents and a good deal of social activity.

15 May: New Moon in Taurus

Of course, your contacts continue to be valuable and important for work but it's basically a time now for you to thoroughly enjoy both life and yourself. Contacts will come to mean journeys, ceremonies, meetings, publicity, gatherings and conferences. Any place/occasion where you're interacting in a group/crowd/gathering is where you're to be found this week! No, not entirely – you could just be going off on 'ownsome lonesome' jaunts with someone special!

22 May: Moon's First Quarter in Virgo

A total about-turn or somersault in terms of activities. Now, it's whatever is secret, surreptitious, even sly and devious, strange, arcane, full of subterfuge and deceit that lies behind your activities. Even money changing hands in secretive deals, scams and scandals. Romance and love affairs too will be conducted in a hush-hush manner, or be beyond the norms of convention and society. You will be concerned with hidden activities – either personal or for your work – and therefore, very, very expensive too.

29 May: Full Moon in Sagittarius

You've had your little flirtation with danger and adventurous living, and now tread the straight and narrow path that leads to house and home, family and domesticity. You decide on a makeover or facelift for your home, as a reflection of your total persona and lifestyle – and a similar exercise with parents, family or children, if you're a parent yourself. Financially, it will be trade and marketing or shopping. All in all, you're buzzing around, full of plans and action.

6 June: Last Quarter in Pisces

Connections and contacts again, but let's call them by a different name now. Ties and partnerships are much more personal, perhaps intimate. There could be a wedding in the family, maybe even yours, if still single. Time and again is the theme of a marriage a recurring feature for Pisceans in the first year of the new millennium! Whatever that may turn out to be, collaborations and partnerships are definitely emphasized.

13 June: New Moon in Gemini

Both work and pleasure fuse for you this week into a harmonious, vibrant and happy unit. In fact, all I really need to say is that you enjoy both in practically equal measure. For 'feckless' Pisceans that's saying a lot about your work front. I do hope I don't have to spell out to you what pleasure means.

Wait though! Ganesha nudges me and says 'Might as well'. It's the twin themes of the personal quest for happiness and the desire to excel at work, as I've already said.

20 June: First Quarter in Virgo

It's only, but only, you the individual that matters this week. And matters are personal, private, subjective. You are in a mood to bare your soul to your mate/spouse/loved one, take him/her into your confidence regarding your plans for the future as well as your present actions. Your own creative instincts are honed and sharpened to awesome perfection so that one of your fondest hopes and dreams could well be on the verge of realization.

28 June: Full Moon in Capricorn

I'm afraid I'll have to take back the words like 'feckless' or 'unambitious', that have crept into the forecasts, if your performance this week is anything to judge by. You will face up to and shoulder some unusually heavy responsibilities, with determination and purpose. That's the way you'll find happiness. Ganesha applauds, and gives you a gift to make things easier – superb creativity so that you perform brilliantly as an individual.

6 July: Last Quarter in Aries

The celestial world you've been floating in will have to be abandoned, for the time being. Pisces is one of the most ethereal of signs but for you now, it's the hard, cold facts of finances that have to be dealt with. Raising capital, investing wisely, trading on the stock exchange will be your main activities. Follow the advice of someone who is both trustworthy as well as streetwise. Pisceans are easy to fool, being trusting themselves in nature. Right now, you need to deal with funds, payments like bonus, alimony or the 'golden handshake', trusts, settlements, hypothecation, insurance.

13 July: New Moon in Cancer

You've taken some wild chances as you played your hunches. Right now, the nail-biting tension and anxiety you might have suffered from will be over and the results will be truly spectacular. Not just the overworked adjective popularly used, but the actual meaning. Which is: all the Ps of power, prosperity, property, progress, position and pelf. Please note what I have put last. It's not because they are less in amount, but perhaps least important for you, as compared to the others listed.

19 July: First Quarter in Libra

You may have been eminently, stupendously successful, but in this quarter, you're eminently, stupendously busy! Home and family, social life, entertaining, career demands and last named but most important – money matters will all demand time, attention, effort. Especially financial matters. They will truly have you in a whirl. And the range of activity will be phenomenal – loans, funds, office, finances, domestic bills, spending, marital resources, even children's fees and extras. So that's the way Ganesha dishes it out to you!

27 July: Full Moon in Aquarius

Another action-packed quarter, ushering in an equally full monthly trend! In fact, Pisces is not a sign that denotes stamina or staying power, so Ganesha sternly prescribes rest, relaxation, health care, dietary control, even a check-up to make sure you're well. What will be demanding, in fact shouting and clamouring for your attention, will be: a) financial matters and a lot of punishingly hard work; b) romantic dalliance; and c) your own spiritual leanings and predilections, prayers and meditation.

4 August: Last Quarter in Taurus

Maybe you've gained the spiritual strength Ganesha wanted you to, or that he has seen you prove yourself. Whatever the reason, he now sends you all the fun and pleasure, parties, games, functions, publicity, ceremonies your heart could possibly have hankered for. And ceremonies could include a wedding, even your own if still single. Perhaps these are the rewards that Ganesha gives you for your good behaviour and even better performance over the last few weeks.

11 August: New Moon in Leo

With all that you've been up to last quarter, will it really be any wonder that your expenses will go through the ceiling? Actually, you don't need me to tell you that, even though the astrological inclinations are what I'm seeing. Also, a certain tiredness, in fact even illness or hospitalization. So, medical expenses as well. I must repeat that it's meditation, prayer, spiritualism that work for you, more than, or at least along with, any doctor's prescription. I could be wrong there, but it's still the way I see it.

18 August: First Quarter in Scorpio

You may have been jolted a bit by all that hit you last week. You certainly realize now that it's your family, close interaction with siblings, relatives and loved ones that are important – vitally so – for you, any way you look at it. What will be equally important, though in an entirely different way, will be research and higher study, advanced learning and education, and pursuit of knowledge and technology. You will be seriously committed to them and sincere in both your attitude and enjoyment of them.

26 August: Full Moon in Pisces

You will be full of determination, strength of purpose, ready to stick your neck out for what you believe is right action for you. This will also apply – and it could be the special gift of the millennium for Pisceans – to your attitude to setbacks, troubles and tribulations. You will handle them beautifully, with much 'grace under pressure'. To turn to more practical matters – financial concerns like funds, taxes, rentals, trade, deals and lucky speculative investment could be important right now.

3 September: Last Quarter in Gemini

You will dazzle with not only the quantum and quantity of hard work you put in, but also its quality. 'Best' is really not an adequate adjective to describe what you give it. There is a reason, in fact two reasons, for this. The astrological one is that a good and powerful trine is formed and the second is your own attitude, moral and ethical values. These are so important that they colour your entire life, your actions and thoughts.

9 September: New Moon in Virgo

There will be a powerful and tremendous shift in focus. Now it's your work, family, life as a whole, the universe as a whole too, that you will be concerned with, and you will strive to create a rare balance, harmony, concord and accord with them and between them all. You will try to reconcile the different pulls. Of course, for you, ties, bonds, attachments will be the total reason for life and living. From this will naturally come great joy in love, marriage, marital harmony and romance, if unattached. A wonder to behold.

16 September: First Quarter in Sagittarius

You have miraculous faith not only in yourself, but in all of mankind, human nature in its total, complex entirety. This kind of cosmic awareness is one of the chief prerogatives of your sign. You will carry on with splendid confidence, self-assurance, downright valour, I'd call it, ready to fight for your beliefs, if required. And these beliefs centre around house, home, family and the quality of life. You will feel that your home is your castle and try to make it safe against any kind of onslaught: land, property, building, construction, renovation, maintenance will be the focus of your activities this quarter.

25 September: Full Moon in Aries

After all the peace and harmony that prevailed, Dame Fortune sends down a bit of a thunderbolt. Financial jugglery, buying, selling, lending, borrowing keep you busy. Much to do with sex, passion too. And most paradoxically, religion, ceremonies and prayers, dealing with the dead as well as the living. I wouldn't be at all surprised if you're confused. Is it any wonder that the stars also predict a slight chance of illness, health hazards, even perhaps an accident, a shock or loss.

2 October: Last Quarter in Cancer

You stuck it out, didn't you? And lived to tell the tale. There will be listeners galore as you party and socialize, as a direct contrast to last week. Family and friends are warm and affectionate, there's love and laughter to chase away the blues you might have felt. Also, there is spectacular success in plans, projects, ventures – both old and new. Good company, good times make you one happy mortal around this time. Ganesha chuckles when I tell him that I feel somewhat envious.

9 October: New Moon in Libra

Personal relationships – just that and nothing else. I mean, what's important for you this quarter, though you'll hardly be doing nothing else. Far from it. All kinds of transactions keep you totally involved – family affairs, entertaining and visitors, and of course, financial transactions too. Business, pleasure, personal life, the works, in fact. You will have to be an acrobat to swing from one to the other, but do it you will. The millennium seems to be giving you large servings of everything.

16 October: First Quarter in Capricorn

It's still personal relationships that are centre stage with you. All the emotions, joys, sorrows, feelings, bonds and ties associated with them will be vital. In fact, if I were to spell them out, I'd put them into three separate compartments: a) your own creativity and talents – and their best use; b) your children, their activities and requirements; and c) domestic affairs and commitments. All of them will require your best and sincerest efforts.

24 October: Full Moon in Taurus

Dreams may come true, hopes and wishes fulfilled about now. It's good, of course, for all the signs but you're one of the luckier ones, Pisceans. Whatever else I go wrong on, I'm almost totally sure of this prediction. What I really wouldn't like to spell out is whether this realization of hopes and dreams will be personal or professional, or both. Normally, for Pisceans, I'd put my money on the first named but the planets can do strange and mysterious things, and nothing surprises me any more.

31 October: Last Quarter in Leo

You will fix your sights firmly on the distant horizon of the future and make your way there firmly and determinedly. You're ready to mould the world, the future, the millennium to your own special design. You will have the inspiration, the flair to make the right moves, choices to modify your perspective, your behaviour, your priorities to get where you want to be. Meanwhile, in the immediate present, there will be, in addition, involvement and performance of rituals and ceremonies, maybe even rites of religion and society.

7 November: New Moon in Scorpio

You'll be bogged down by the expenses you have to cope with. They could be connected to the last sentence of the previous forecast. You may feel lonely, perhaps even abandoned, as you struggle to cope. It's your joyous interaction with children that will give you solace and strength. In fact, they could enjoy marvellous success, especially at interviews and examinations. And so do you. In fact, you will really have a lot to be happy about. Positive thinking will also help you overcome your angst, loneliness, Weltschmertz (world weariness). In any case, Pisces makes its natives prone to this, along with the soft-bellied Cancerians, including me too.

15 November: First Quarter in Aquarius

You're eager, willing, keen to reach out a helping hand to others, with absolutely no hidden agenda or ulterior motive. It just makes you feel good, and helps you equally. Some of the most dedicated activists and social workers come from your sign. You'll certainly be very, very busy with sheer hard work. You will struggle to create time for your dependents, projects, pets but you'll do it. Take it easy when you can.

23 November: Full Moon in Gemini

You will earn, and truly merit the respect of others. Somehow, that doesn't surprise me at all. You will grow and develop tremendously as a human being – spectacularly so. In more concrete terms there could be a promotion, raise, perks, greater job benefits, awards and rewards, public recognition, personal satisfaction. I hope you feel suitably grateful to Ganesha for this.

30 November: Last Quarter in Virgo

It's yourself you want to improve, your own lot you want to better. It could also be the effect of all that's happened to you last week. Whatever the reason, you embark on this self-enhancement drive as a single-point programme. As is always the case with Pisces, the motivating factor is your own idealism, the lofty ideas and sentiments that compel you to do this. And do it you will. Actually, in doing so, you help others and benefit them.

7 December: New Moon in Sagittarius

All that you embark on will have the Midas touch, but not with the same results as King Midas. There will be brightness and gaiety on the domestic scene, success in business ventures and the office or workplace, marvellous home conditions and family life. Not only is it a truly mind-blowing experience, it also creates well-being. This is actually and truly the gift of the millennium for you. It was just a little late in coming, but now it's here to stay. You have won your spurs the hard way in the battle of life, and nobody can take them away from you.

15 December: First Quarter in Pisces

It doesn't surprise me at all to predict what Ganesha tells me to, for you Pisceans in this week, the one to come, and for the year 2019. I'm sure even you will consider it more or less a given in the present scenario. People surround you, physically and with love, and caring and sharing. Romance and love, of course, also success in social life, at meetings, powwows and tête-è-tête, on a larger canvas at conferences and business gatherings.

22 December: Full Moon in Cancer

It's time to devote your attention to home, domesticity, parents. You will have to work at being more tactful and less neurotic and ready to fly off the handle. Pisceans rarely hold a grudge, and are always willing not only to forgive and forget, but admit their own faults and shortcomings. You will feel the need to plan for your future, whether it's planning for a home, house, even pied-à-terre (a home away from home, as I love to call it). In that respect, you feel that your home is your stronghold, the source of your strength, your roots, your origin.

29 December: Last Quarter in Libra

The year 2018 ends on such a positive and upbeat note that you'll know you're going places. In fact, there's no stopping you, with your confidence and determination at an all-time high. You know that it's only practical and natural to realize that you only have to look ahead with hope and zest for all that you'll be doing. You will be totally justified in this belief, Ganesha says it's so. After all, just as there's no going back to the old millennium when the new one has dawned, so also for you. What a promise from Ganesha!

Achievements 2018

By the grace of Lord Ganesh, my son Nastur found patrons in Shri Raj Kumar Jatia and his son, Shri Adarsh Jatia, the owners of Four Seasons, Mumbai, and Provenance Four Seasons Private Residences. May patience and hard work take my son to the top of the world where Shri Raj Kumar Jatia stands like a shining star. Nastur was graciously invited by the noble business tycoon, Byram Avari, of Avari Group of Hotels, Karachi, and his wife, Goshpi Avari, to attend their fiftieth wedding anniversary.

I bless prosperity upon Prayush Poddar, his father and his family. May his company, AMP Universal Realty Pvt. Ltd, prosper. He has been like a son to me.

May the grace of Lord Ganesha bless Police Commissioner Anupam Singh Gehlot of Rajkot. He has always stood by my family, in good times and bad. Peace and prosperity prevail in Rajkot because of his sincere efforts.

BJP National vice-president and Rajya Sabha member, Vinay Sahasrabuddhe is a very fine and noble gentleman. He was gracious enough to arrange a meeting with Maharashtra chief minister Devendra Fadnavis, who was dynamic and touched by the divine.

Body Language

Ganesha believed astrology to be all about behaviour, relationships and how to handle them. Therefore, the guidelines given below should help you to understand yourself and others. Any information that adds to the knowledge of oneself is always welcome. Here are some examples of body language and its possible interpretations:

POSITIVE VIBES

- Open arms and hands: open and receptive

- Leaning forward: interested in conversation

- Smiling or attempting to be humorous: friendly

- Eye contact with occasional, natural breaks in the stare: focused and curious

- Nodding while listening: attentive and alert

- Open palms: approachable and trusting

- Gesturing with hands while talking: genuinely involved in the conversation

- Upright shoulders: positivity

NEGATIVE VIBES

- Crossed arms and/or legs: closed off, defensive, reserved or suspicious

- Standing with hands inside the pockets: unsure or suspicious

- Fidgeting, running one's tongue along one's teeth, playing with hair or jewellery or tapping feet: nervous and/or bored

- Lack of eye contact or staring too intently and unblinkingly: untrustworthy

- Leaning back: uncomfortable

- Clasping hands behind the head while leaning back: seeking power

- Drooping shoulders: unsure

Colours of Life

Ganesha believes that life is like a rainbow. Life is like nature, full of abundance and variety. The best part of it is you can actually experiment with the colours given below and have fun. Here, we combine abundance and a variety of colours for joy, use, experience.

- **Energetic:** Red
- **Sporty:** Red, orange
- **Exuberant:** Orange
- **Active:** Orange, yellow
- **Modern:** Yellow
- **Invigorating:** Green, yellow
- **Sunny:** Green, yellow
- **Fresh:** Green
- **Luminous:** Blue, Green
- **Hypnotic:** Blue
- **Regal:** Blue, violet
- **Exotic:** Violet
- **Playful:** Red, orange, violet, yellow
- **Vibrant:** Green, red

(Your astrologer admits that this colour system is *not* his own.)

Important Dates

I have always believed that the fear of failure has never led to advancement of knowledge. These dates and directions may differ from the various trends and forecasts mentioned elsewhere in the book. A different direction is being pursued here. This is a totally different ball game. This is to be taken as an experiment on a mass scale with the readers themselves as guinea pigs (willingly, I hope).

Please remember, as a rule, your birth month and the seventh month from it (including itself) will be hectic. For example, if your birth month is March, the seventh from it will be September. There will be tremendous franticness in both these months.

ARIES

January: 3–4, 8–9, 11–15, 17–18, 21–22, 25–27, 30–31
February: 1, 4–6, 9–10, 13–15, 18–19, 22–23, 27–28
March: 3–4, 7–9, 12–13, 16–17, 20–21, 25–26, 30–31
April: 4–5, 8–9, 12–13, 16–17, 20–21, 25–26, 30–31
May: 1–2, 5–6, 9–11, 14–15, 19–20, 24–25, 28–30
June: 2–3, 6–7, 10–11, 15–16, 20–21, 25–26, 29–30
July: 2–3, 6–7, 10–11, 15–16, 20–21, 25–26, 28–30
August: 1, 4–5, 8–10, 13–15, 19–20, 23–24, 27–29
September: 1, 5–6, 10–11, 15–16, 19–20, 23–24, 27–29

October: 2–3, 7–8, 12–13, 16–17, 21–22, 25–26, 29–31

November: 3–5, 8–9, 13–14, 17–18, 21–22, 26–27

December: 1–2, 6–7, 10–11, 14–15, 18–20 (everything meets during 18–20 December, it is the focal point), 23–24, 28–29

Special Note: For Aries, February is the launch pad to the entire year.

TAURUS

January: 1–2, 5–7, 10–12, 15–16, 19–20, 23–24, 28–29

February: 2–3, 7–8, 11–12. 16–17, 20–21, 24–26, 29

March: 1–28, 5–6, 10–11, 14–15, 18–19, 22–24, 27–29

April: 1–3, 6–7, 10–11, 14–16, 19–20, 24–25, 29–30

May: 3–4, 7–8, 12–13, 16–18 (matters come to a boil now), 22–23, 26–27, 31

June: 1, 4–5, 8–9, 12–14, 17–19, 22–24, 27–28

July: 2–3 (springboard for family, food, fraternity, friendship), 6–7, 10–12, 15–16, 20–22, 25–26, 29–30

August: 2–3, 6–7, 11–12, 16–18, 21–22, 26–28, 30–31

September: 3–4, 8–9, 13–14, 17–19, 22–23, 26–27, 30

October: 1, 5–6, 10–11, 15–16, 20–21, 23–25, 28–30

November: 1–2, 6–7, 10–12, 15–16, 19–20, 23–25, 28–30

December: 3–5, 8–9, 12–13, 16–17, 20–22, 25–27, 30–31.

GEMINI

January: 3–4, 8–9, 13–14, 17–8, 21–22, 25–27, 30–31

February: 1, 4–6, 9–10, 13–15, 18–19, 22–23, 27–28 (February is the time for planning the future)

March: 3–4, 8–9, 12–13, 16–18, 21–22, 25–27, 30–31

April: 4–5, 8–9, 12–13,17–18, 21–23, 26–28

May: 5–6, 9–11, 14–15, 19–20 24–25, 28–30

June: 2–3, 6–7, 10–11, 15–16, 20–21, 25–26, 29–30 (June will be synonymous with joy)

July: 3–4, 7–9, 12–14, 17–19, 22–23, 27–28, 31

August: 1, 4–5, 8–10, 13–15, 18–20, 23–24, 27–28, 30–31

September: 5–6, 10–11, 15–16, 19–20, 23–24, 27–29

October: 2–3, 7–8, 12–13, 16–17, 21–22, 25–26, 29–31, (children and ideas may take up your time and energy)

November: 3–5, 8–9, 13–14, 17–18, 21–22, 26–27

December: 1–2, 6–7, 10–11, 14–15, 18–20, 23–24, 28–29

Special Note: From the number of stars in this month you clever, nibble-witted Geminis will find August to be pivotal for contacts, contracts, relationships, favours, and obligations. Attachments and ties made around or after June will run into the next year and may last your whole life.

CANCER

January: 1–2, 5–7, 10–12, 15–16, 19–20, 23–24, 28–29

February: 2–3, 7–8, 11–12, 16–17, 20–21, 24–26, 29

March: 1–2, 5–6, 10–11, 14–15, 18–19, 22–24, 27–29

April: 1–3, 6–7, 10–11, 14–16, 19–20, 24–25, 29–30.

May: 3–4, 7–8 12–13, 16–18, 21–23, 26–27, 31

June: 4–5, 8–9 , 12–14, 17–19, 22–24, 27–28

July: 1–2, 5–6, 10–11, 15–16, 20–21, 24–26, 29–30

August: 2–3, 6–7, 11–12,16–17, 21–22, 25–26, 29–30

September: 2–4, 7–9, 12–14, 17–18, 21–11, 25–26, 30

October: 1, 4–6, 9–11, 14–15, 18–20, 23–24, 27–28
November: 1–2, 6–7, 10–11, 15–16, 19–20, 23–25, 28–30
December: 3–5, 8–9, 10–13, 16–17, 21–11, 25–27, 30–31

Special Note: January and March are always the hub or central force from where the spokes of relationships, contacts, communication, and ties start for Cancerians. May and November are the months whirling in the social whirligig. By mixing with people, you multiply your chances of success and happiness. In July, seventy out of 100 times the birth month becomes exceptionally important for luck, changes, relationships. Usually, but not always, it will be one of the most powerful months. September is essential for making contacts, communicating, contracts and tie-ins. The last week of December will be a mighty preparation for reaching out to people and places in 2018.

LEO
January: 3–4, 8–9, 13–14, 17–18, 21–22, 25–27
February: 4–6, 9–10, 13–15, 18–19, 22–23, 27–29
March: 3–4, 7–9, 12–13
April: 1–2, 11–13, 19–20, 23–25, 28–29
May: 3–4, 8–10, 16–17, 20–21, 25–26, 30–31
June: 4–6, 8–9, 16–18, 21–22, 26–27
July: 1–2, 5–6, 10–11, 14–15, 18–20, 28–29
August: 2–3, 6–7, 9–12, 15–16, 19–21, 23–26, 29–30
September: 1–3, 6–8, 11–12, 16–17, 21–22, 25–26, 29–30
October: 2–3, 7–8, 12–13, 16–178, 21–22, 26–27
November: 3–5, 8–9, 13–14, 17–18, 21–22, 25–26, 29–31
December: 1–2, 6–7, 10–11, 14–15, 18–20, 23–24, 28–29

Special Note: For Leos, February, though slightly difficult, is an important gateway for meeting people and bonding with dear ones. Trips are likely in this month. Though August is your birth month and you will have a sense of power, you must be careful not to antagonize people, particularly those dear to you. A little diplomacy will grease the creaking wheels of relationships. Surprisingly, expect sudden and/or secret good fortune. For any sort of crowd-pulling activity, popularity or publicity, October and November make a single unit. December is for having a ball. Taureans, Leos, Scorpios and Aquarians will have 'kisses and kicks, bouquets and brickbats' in all relationships this year. The reason is that Uranus (the planet of rebellion and unforeseen events), Neptune (signifying delusion and deceit), Saturn (symbolizing sorrow, and karma) are in a bad position or placing, particularly for these four signs. Even then, the grace of Ganesha/Allah/Christ/Buddha will be the saviour. The months of February, May, August and November are the ones when the good and the bad are likely to happen. Load your gun and be ready.

VIRGO

January: 1–2, 5–7, 10–12, 15–16, 19–20, 23–24, 28–29
February: 2–3, 7–8, 11–12, 16–17, 20–21, 24–26, 29
March: 1–2, 5–6, 10–11 14–15, 18–19, 22–24, 27–29
April: 1–3, 6–7, 10–11, 14–16, 19–20, 24–25, 29–30
May: 3–4, 7–8, 12–13, 16–18, 21–23, 26–27, 31
June: 1, 4–5, 8–9, 12–14, 17–19, 22–23, 27–28
July: 1–2, 6–7, 10–12, 15–16, 20–21, 24–26, 29–30
August: 2–3, 6–7, 11–13, 16–18, 21–22, 25–26, 29–31

September: 2–4, 7–9, 12–14, 17–18, 21–22, 25–26, 30
October: 1, 4–6, 9–11, 14–15, 18–20, 23–26 (very important), 30–31
November: 1–2, 6–7, 10–12, 15–16, 19–20, 23–25, 28–30
December: 3–5, 8–9, 12–13, 16–17, 20–24, 26–27 30–31

Special Note: The reason, dear Virgos, for so many important dates in January is that you will start the year in style. You will have the advantage of being in the fast lane of love, life and laughter. See that your tentacles catch and hold on to all those you can count on. Children will give you immense satisfaction. This March, you will travel and touch the lives of people. Importantly, you will drop your guard and shed your inhibitions. In May, despite delays and hesitations, your heart will sympathize and be in symphony with others. This is the time to plan your future. The people you meet in your working life will influence you the most is June. July is the meeting point of home and the outside wide world of privacy and group activity. For Virgos, September will be a great month. You move into top gear on 23 October. The last days of December find you fit, charming, romantic and, more importantly, willing to take chances.

LIBRA

January: 8–10, 13–15, 18–19, 22–23, 26–27, 31
February: 1, 4–6, 10–11, 14–15, 22–23, 27–28
March: 3–4, 7–9, 12–13, 16–17, 20–21, 30–31
April: 3–5, 8–9, 12–13, 17–18, 20–22, 26–28
May: 5–6, 9–11, 14–15, 19–20, 24–25, 28–30
June: 2–3, 6–7, 10–11,15–16, 20–21, 25–26, 29–30
July: 3–4, 6–7, 10—11, 15–16, 20–21, 25–26, 29–30

August: 1, 4–5, 8–10, 13–15, 18–20, 23–24, 27–28, 31

September: 1, 4–6, 11–13, 15–17, 20–21, 24–25, 27–29

October: 6–8, 12–13, 16–17, 21–22, 24–26, 28–30

November: 2–4, 7–98, 13–14, 17–18, 21–23, 27–29

December: 1–2, 6–7, 10–11, 14–15, 18–20, 23–24, 28–29

Special Note: In January, you will interact with people at home and outside. The period from 21 January to 23 February and from 21 March to 21 April are very special. During 21 May to 20 June expect contacts and travel. Expect friendships and socializing during 21 July to 21 August. From 21 September to 21 October, it will be truly hectic and a time to focus on relationships. From 21 November to 21 December, it is time for trips and ties, the two Ts.

SCORPIO

January: 5–7, 10–12. 15–16, 23–24, 23–24, 28–29

February: 2–3,7–8, 11–12, 16–17, 20–21, 24–26, 29

March: 1–2, 5–6,10–11, 14–15, 18–19, 22–24, 27–30

April: 1–3, 6–7, 10–11, 14–16, 19–20, 24–25, 29–30

May: 3–4, 6–7, 12–138, 16–18, 21–23, 26–27, 31

June: 1, 4–5, 8–9, 12–14, 17–19, 22–24, 27–28

July: 1–2, 5–6, 10–11, 15–16, 24–26, 29–30

August: 2–3, 6–7, 10–12, 15–16, 19–20, 23–25, 28–29

September: 2–4 7–9, 12–14, 17–18, 25–26, 30

October: 1, 4–6, 9–11, 14–15, 18–20, 23–24, 27–28

November: 1–2, 6–7, 10–12, 15–16, 24–26, 29–30

December: 3–5, 7–9, 13–14, 16–17, 21–23, 25–27, 30–31

Special Note: In January, you will be off to a very quick start and therefore interacting with people; journeys have added importance. In May, your relationships will be both sweet and sour, spicy and bitter. You are duly warned. A lot of things happen in July: a lot of activity, thus a lot of stars. Don't push people too hard or it will boomerang in August. A wish-fulfilment is possible. Stop being friendly and give that devilish Scorpio smile with a raised eyebrow.

SAGITTARIUS

January: 3–4, 8–9, 13–14, 17–18, 21–22, 25–26, 30–31
February: 1, 4–5, 9–10, 13–14, 18–19, 22–23, 27–28
March: 3–5, 7–9, 12–13, 16–17, 20–21, 25–26, 30–31
April: 4–5, 8–9, 12–13, 17–18, 21–28, 26–27
May: 1–3, 5–6, 10–11, 14–15, 19–20, 25–26, 28–30
June: 2–3, 6–7, 10–11, 15–16, 20–21, 25–26, 28–30
July: 2–4, 7–9, 12–14, 18–20, 22–24, 27–28, 31
August: 1, 4–5, 8–9, 12–14, 18–20, 23–24, 27–28, 31
September: 1–2, 5–6, 10–11, 15–16, 19–20, 23–24, 27–29
October: 2–3, 7–8, 12–13, 16–17, 21–22,25–26, 29–31
November: 3–5, 8–9, 13–14, 17–18, 21–22, 26–27
December: 1–2, 6–7, 10–11, 14–15, 18–20, 23–24, 28–29

Special Note: For you, Sagittarians, June and onwards will be important for romance, collaborations, conferences and connections.

CAPRICORN

January: 1–2, 5–7, 10–11, 15–16, 19–20, 23–24, 28–29
February: 2–3, 7–8, 11–12, 16–17, 20–21, 24–25, 29

March: 1, 5–6, 10–11, 14–15, 18–19, 22–24, 27–29
April: 1–3, 6–7, 10–11, 14–16, 19–20, 24–25, 29–30
May: 2–3, 7–8, 12–13, 16–18, 21–23, 26–27, 31
June: 1, 4–5, 8–9, 12–14, 17–19, 22–24, 27–28
July: 1–2, 10–11, 15–16, 20–21, 24–26, 29–30
September: 2–4, 7–9, 12–14, 17–18, 21–22, 25–26, 30
October: 1, 4–6, 9–11, 14–15, 18–20,23–24, 27–28
November: 1–2, 5–6, 10–11, 15–16, 19–20, 23–25, 28–30
December: 2–4, 7–9, 11–13, 17–19, 22–23, 24–27, 29–31

Special Note: During May, July, September and November there will be a blizzard and a blitzkrieg in your relationships. Do not worry. You will make more friends than enemies. That's the bottom line and nobody understands it better than Capricorns, Taureans and Virgoans.

AQUARIUS
January: 3–4, 8–9, 13–14, 17–18, 21–11, 25–27, 30–31
February: 1, 4–6, 9–10, 13–15, 18–19, 22–23, 27–28
March: 3–4, 7–9, 12–13, 16–17, 20–21, 25–26, 30–31
April: 4–5, 8–9, 12–13, 16–17, 20–21, 25–26, 30–31
May: 3–4, 9–11, 14–15, 19–20, 24–25, 28–30
June: 2–3, 6–7, 10–11, 15–16, 20–21, 25–26, 29–30
July: 3–4, 7–9, 12–13, 17–18, 21–23, 26–28
August:1, 4–5, 8–10, 13–15, 18–19, 23–24, 27–28, 31
September: 1, 5–6, 10–11, 15–16, 19–20, 23–24, 27–29
October: 2–3, 7–8, 12–13, 16–17, 21–22, 25–26, 29–30
November: 3–5, 8–9, 13–14, 17–18, 21–22, 26–27
December: 1–2, 5–6, 10–11, 14–15, 18–20, 23–24, 28–29

PISCES

January: 1–2, 4–7, 10–12, 15–16, 19–20, 23–24, 28–29
February: 2–3, 7–8, 11–12, 16–17, 20–21, 24–26, 29
March: 1–2, 5–6, 10–11, 14–15, 18–19, 22–24, 27–29
April: 4–5, 8–9, 14–16, 18–19, 22–24, 27–29
May: 3–4, 7–8, 12–13, 16–18, 21–23, 26–27, 31
June: 1, 4–5, 8–9, 12–14, 17–19, 22–24, 27–28
July: 1–2, 4–5, 10–11, 15–16, 20–21, 24–26, 29–30
August: 2–3, 6–7, 11–12, 13–17, 21–22, 25–26, 29–30
September: 2–4, 7–9, 12–14, 17–18, 21–22, 25–26, 30
October: 1, 4–6, 9–11, 14–16, 19–20, 23–25, 28–30
November: 1–2, 6–7, 10–12, 15–16, 19–20, 23–25, 28–30
December: 3–5, 8–9, 12–13, 16–17, 20–22, 24–27, 30–31

Special Note: Through journey and communication as well as short distances which require commuting and motoring, you will meet not only people but the love of your life too. January, March, May, September, November, should be wildly exciting.

Secret of Life

❧

Ganesha (whom you may refer to as Allah/Christ/Zoroaster or by any other name) is the ignition key of life's car. To start and launch in the name of Ganesha is to assure success and glory. The power, the dazzling light to see visions, have prophetic dreams, and are all bestowed upon us by Ganesha.

Ganesha says the secret of life is in the ability to change with the changing times. In other words, it is the ability to adapt and adjust to situations, conditions, surroundings, climate change, relationships, and science and technology. His second secret is to keep an open mind. Others are most welcome to their own opinion. The third and final secret is to be true to yourself.

Success Secret of No. 17

Ganesha says the secret of life and astrology is to 'Observe! Observe! Observe!' Angela Merkel of Germany, our own Narendra Modi, former US first lady Michelle Obama, and Muhammad Ali, the world's greatest boxer, were all born on the seventeenth days of their birth months. Here is a picture of the tarot card of number seventeen, called the 'Star'. We can see a lady pouring water on the Earth and providing nourishment. To me the lady is the symbol of the great feminine principle which rules the entire world. There are seven stars in the card. As we all know, seven is the mystical number of spirituality, growth and development.

Narendra Modi, 17 September

Michelle Obama, 17 January

Angela Merkel, 17 July

Muhammad Ali, 17 January

To observe is to see completely and carefully. If you observe the above, you will find that all these four individuals are born on the seventeenth. Secondly, the first alphabet of either the first name or the surname in each case is 'M'. The tarot card points towards a great and powerful destiny. Therefore, for all these reasons I believe that the number seventeen and the letter 'M' go with greatness and glory. Yes, I agree that it may not hold true for all the persons born on the seventeenth of various months. I am open-minded.

Is it but a coincidence or is it fate and destiny? I leave it to you to decide.

World Horoscope 2018

Ganesha says cooking is an art. The challenge lies in the ever-changing nature of the ingredients, the temperature, the flavour, the aroma and the very style of cooking.

The ingredients are: artificial intelligence; healing broken bodies, mind, and spirit (most important); managerial skills of a high order; immense strides in medicine and specially brain power; space travel; robots; biopharmaceuticals; origin of life; God vs technology; climate change; and finally the marriage of technology and humanity.

Let me put it in very simple terms. The years from 2018 to 2020 will have both revolution and evolution. Change is the only constant law of nature. Not only will we survive, we will also prevail. The planets responsible for this constant change in direction are Jupiter, Saturn and Pluto. Jupiter means prosperity, Saturn means inevitable changes and Pluto means drastic and unavoidable situations and effects. These three planets are the trio of the cardinal, ambitious, ruthless sign of duty and responsibility: Capricorn. In short, Capricorn is the father who uses a big stick for others but unhappily not for himself. That is the comedy and the tragedy of the Capricorn sign.

As I have said earlier, this is not the right time for Donald Trump. His world view is one that is corrupted by imagination, illusion and, sometimes, hallucination. The Capricorn North Korean President Kim Jong-un will face terrible times and will be completely defeated in the end by fate. Vladimir Putin of Russia and Theresa May of the UK will find it very difficult to hold on to power. Angela Merkel of Germany is simply wonderful and effective. There is a distinct possibility of a settlement or an understanding between the Jews and the Muslims in 2018 itself. God bless them both. Changes in the regimes in Pakistan and the UK appear certain. In the words of Paul Brenton, 'There is peace behind the tumult, goodness behind the evil, happiness behind the agony.' Nobody has a monopoly over truth, love, justice, mercy, kindness and happiness.

India is certainly tolerant up to a certain extent, but it would be wise, practical and necessary to be much more tolerant and far less rigid and orthodox. Water recycling and the treatment of sewage will be a big changer for our country in 2018 and 2019. It will lead to happiness. I say this in all humility and love for Bharat Mata as I am her child. I certainly bow my head at the feet of Bharat Mata. India comes under the planet of Saturn causing changes that are radical, effective, certain. Our Narendra Modi will hold his own against the world. But India will undergo numerous changes, a few of them could be painful but are necessary in the bigger scheme of events. Not religion but responsibility, duty and development will be the three salient features of India in the coming years.

To be happy we must keep an open mind. Perhaps, I say perhaps the best years will be 2018 and 2021. The year 2021 is most certainly the one when science and technology reign supreme and change the very fabric and direction of all of us. Possibly this is the greatest prediction your humble Ganesha devotee will ever make.

Salute and Tribute

A salute and tribute to the following people:

- Gujarat chief minister Vijay Rupani, in whom I saw a perfect balance in the lines of fate, head and heart on his palms. A great heart and a finely tuned mind.

- Philanthropist and naturalist Firdoz Khambhatta, a dangerously handsome, sharp and brilliant man.

- The lovely Meher Medora, firm of purpose and understanding and sympathetic of heart.

- Aravind Mothi and his sister, Anu Mothi, for offering to make a documentary on my life.

- Hotelier Raj Kumar Jatia for his hospitality and courtesy.

- Behram Mehta for his business acumen fused with immense humility and humanity.

- Jay Shah, son of BJP president Amit Shah, for coming to my house and seeking the blessings of all the mighty spirits and energies of each and every religion.

- The very cultured, civilized, and well-informed education minister of Gujarat, Shri Bhupendra Chudasma for his wisdom as well as his faith in Ganesha.

- Usha Nair, Dr Sunny Shah, Nashit Afroze and their team at the International Human Rights Council for services rendered to NGOs all over the world. I was very humbled to receive a trophy from them, one I shall always treasure.

- Prince Lakshyaraj of Udaipur for his constant endeavour to help thousands of people through education, NGOs and by example for leading an exemplary life.

- My personal blessings by calling upon all the energies of the world to bless my adopted son Chirag and his fiancée Nikita. They are gems.

- I bow very humbly to my guru, Vashishth Mehta, for coaching me across the path of astrology and spirituality.

- Kudos to Neeraj Bajaj, the son of my late friend and patron Ramkrishna Bajaj, and Dadi Mistry for helping the needy, the weak and the helpless in every possible way. Both are truly magnanimous people.

- Raja Vikram Singh of Jambughoda for his humour and resounding laughter. No wonder his Jambughoda resort is doing immensely well.

- Just as this book is going to press, I met Shiroy and his fiancée, Avasti. Avasti specializes in fashion. Shiroy is an absolute gentleman.

- Lastly, I salute and pay my tribute to all those who seek and serve the cause of peace and goodwill to humanity. To me this is certainly the final word.

About the Author

Born on 11 July 1931, Bejan Daruwalla lives with his wife and their three children. Now, eighty-six years old, he is regarded as one of the hundred greatest astrologers of the last century, as acknowledged by *The Millennium Book of Prophecy* (HarperCollins), having accurately predicted the electoral victory of Narendra Modi at the Kanoria Art Centre, Ahmedabad, on 29 March 2012. Bejan featured on *Hard Talk India* on BBC in August 1999. On 10 December 2010, Bejan was featured in *The Job: Corporate Astrologer* in London's *Financial Times*. Bejan was also awarded the Dr Babasaheb Ambedkar Noble Award on 19 April 2017. Giving Bejan more joy and material achievement was shaking hands with His Holiness the Dalai Lama in December 2013, a moment unforgotten and overwhelming. Bejan has one firm belief: tolerance. He believes everyone has the right to their own ideas and opinions; the perspective of others, even and especially if it differs from one's own, must always be respected.

Important Announcement

Our Ganesha devotee Bejan Daruwalla has moved from Mumbai to Ahmedabad. His Ahmedabad address is:

Bejan Daruwalla
Astrologer and Columnist
C/o Nastur Daruwalla
A-5, Spectrum Towers
Opposite Police Stadium
Shahibag
Ahmedabad 380004
India

Telephone
079-32954387
09825470377
08141234275

Email
info@bejandaruwalla.com
bejandaruwalla@rediffmail.com

Website: www.bejandaruwalla.com